D0081583

Arts, Health and Well-Being

This important book develops a critical understanding of the bridging of arts and health domains, drawing on models and perspectives from social sciences to develop the case for arts and health as a social movement. This interdisciplinary perspective offers a new research agenda that can help to inform future developments and sustainability in arts, health and well-being.

Daykin begins with an overview of the current evidence base and a review of current challenges for research, policy and practice. Later chapters explore the international field of health and the arts; arts, with well-being as a social movement; and boundary work and the role of boundary objects in the field. This book also includes sections summarising research findings and evidence in arts and health research and examples from specific research projects conducted by the author, chosen to highlight particularly widespread challenges across many arts, health and well-being contexts.

Arts, Health and Well-Being: A Critical Perspective on Research, Policy and Practice is valuable reading for students in sociology, psychology, social work, nursing, psychiatry, creative and performing arts, public health and policymakers and practitioners in these fields.

Norma Daykin is Professor in New Social Research at Tampere University, Finland, Professor Emerita in Arts in Health at the University of the West of England, UK, and a visiting Professor in Arts as Wellbeing at the University of Winchester, UK. She is a social scientist and musician known for her award-winning research on arts, health and well-being. Her research has spanned a wide range of methodologies and topics, from the impact of hospital design on patient well-being through to the impact of participatory arts in mental health, primary care, community and justice settings.

Arts, Health and Well-Being
A Critical Perspective on Research, Policy and Practice

Norma Daykin

Routledge
Taylor & Francis Group

LONDON AND NEW YORK

First published 2020
by Routledge
2 Park Square, Milton Park, Abingdon, Oxon OX14 4RN

and by Routledge
52 Vanderbilt Avenue, New York, NY 10017

Routledge is an imprint of the Taylor & Francis Group, an informa business

British Library Cataloguing-in-Publication Data
A catalogue record for this book is available from the British Library

Library of Congress Cataloging-in-Publication Data
A catalog record has been requested for this book

ISBN: 978-0-367-40417-8 (hbk)
ISBN: 978-0-429-35604-9 (ebk)

Typeset in Times New Roman
by codeMantra

Contents

1 Introduction

The last 20 years have seen a growing interest and burgeoning evidence of the health and well-being impacts of arts such as music, visual arts, drama, creative writing and other activities. During this period, artists have joined together with researchers, health professionals and policy makers to explore the connections between arts, health and well-being. An international evidence base is expanding in volume and growing in quality, while regional, national and international networks have been established to share knowledge and support the development of policy and practice. Senior policy makers have spoken in support of integrating arts and creativity at every stage of healthcare. However, significant challenges need to be addressed before such a goal can become a reality.

Combining arts and health is seen as a potential solution to demographic and social challenges that have transformed experiences of health and disease, often revealing the limitations of technological medicine. The power of arts and creativity have been invoked to address a range of policy agendas, including supporting marginalised communities and addressing well-being inequalities. However, 'arts' and 'health' are characterised by separate histories, organisational practices, cultural traditions, professional roles and identities, and each domain faces particular challenges in contemporary society. The task of overcoming these divisions in order to develop a common vision and purpose is not straightforward.

Two related premises underline this book. First, the development of healthcare knowledge is not a neutral scientific process but is shaped by political governance, regulation and social action [1]. This perspective draws on writings on the sociology of professions by researchers such as Margaret Stacey, who discusses the changes in society, including population growth, increased wealth, advances in technology, changing attitudes and a growth in the regulatory functions of the state, which allowed the consolidation of professional power and the establishment of Western Scientific Medicine (WSM) as the dominant form of health-care provision in Europe [2]. The second premise of this book is that the development of artistic knowledge and practice is similarly embedded in social and political relations. Hence, artistic quality cannot 'speak for itself'; rather, the production and reception of artwork is a social process embedded in interaction and influenced by hierarchies such as class, gender, ethnicity, caste and sexual identity [3–5].

This book develops a critical understanding of the bridging of arts and health domains, beginning with an overview of the current evidence base and a review of current challenges for research, policy and practice. I draw on models and perspectives from social sciences to develop the case for arts and health as a social movement, exploring boundary work and the role of boundary objects in arts, health and well-being. These theories offer a new research agenda that can help to inform future developments and sustainability in arts, health and well-being.

Limits to medicine

Since the 1960s, scientific medicine, which had dominated under-standing of health and disease from after the European Enlightenment until the middle of the 20th century, has been subjected to sustained critique.

The basis of scientific medicine in 'Cartesian dualism', the belief that mind and body are separate entities, has led to mechanistic and reductionist approaches to health problems [4]. Healthcare systems organised around the principles of scientific medicine were increasingly questioned by economists, sociologists, feminists, professional groups and complementary therapists [5,6]. Radical doctors such as Ivan Illich pointed to modern medicine's iatrogenic effects, which include not just the damage done by ineffective or unsafe treatments but also broader harms inflicted by consumerism and attempts to control and deny essential human experiences of dealing with death, pain and sickness [7]. Public health researchers demonstrated the contribution that social and environmental factors, such as improvements in hygiene and income distribution, have made to population health improvements [8].

More recently, it has been estimated that less than 10% of what affects our health and well-being comes from access to health-care [9]. Current health and care challenges stem from demographic and social trends, with increases in life expectancy not necessarily translating into healthy lives in later years. Throughout the life course, the prevalence of chronic physical and mental ill health is at unprecedented levels, compounded by widening health inequalities causing a disproportionate burden of ill health to be borne by people on low incomes [10]. These conditions create mounting pressure on health services, combined with rising care costs and difficulties in recruiting and retaining staff. There is a growing consensus that health services cannot be held solely accountable for the nation's health and that a shift in emphasis is needed towards prevention. Many arts and health projects have developed from a recognition of the limits of medical models of health and care, particularly in areas such as chronic illness and dementia, where medical solutions are unlikely to address needs. Nevertheless, biomedical research still maintains a dominant position in many areas of research, regulation and healthcare practice.

Arts and cultural challenges

A shift in thinking within the arts coincided with these changing perspectives on health and disease away from scientific medicine towards more holistic models of health and care. The impetus for what has been described as a social movement of arts, health and well-being has been traced to the emergence of community arts in the 1960s, which challenged the role of art in society, particularly the perception of 'high art' as aloof and disconnected from the problems of ordinary people [11]. The arts and health movement challenges fundamental ideas about the nature of creativity that have shaped the development of arts in modern European societies. For example, during the Romantic period, the artist was held separate from society, visionary but marginalised, heroic but tragically unrecognised [12,13]. The influence of these ideas, together with more recent trends towards commercialism and commodification, has perpetuated an elitist and de-contextualised view of the arts and fostered unhelpful stereotypes that isolate artists, making it difficult for them to organise, find support for their own well-being and command appropriate financial rewards for their work [14].

While these ideas have been challenged by those favouring socially engaged models of arts practice, their influence can still be seen, for example, in debates about artistic quality. There is sometimes a presumption that community arts and arts for health and well-being are 'instrumental' activities lacking in quality. Yet artistic quality is a complex and subjective phenomenon that is only just beginning to be critically discussed and mapped within the arts sector. The role of artistic quality in arts and health practice has not been well understood, and this area has sometimes been overlooked by practitioners and service delivery organisations as well as researchers, whose attention and efforts have been consumed by seeking to find ways to demonstrate health and well-being outcomes and address medically based hierarchies of evidence.

Outline of this book

This book is in two parts. Part 1 begins with a discussion of the development of the field of arts, health and well-being in Chapter 2 and an overview of research and evidence in Chapter 3. Research challenges are discussed, drawing on case studies of visual arts and music in health and community contexts (Chapter 4). While the quality of research in the field is continually improving, these chapters reveal underlying problems and questions that cannot be addressed through methodologies alone. Part 2 explores theories from social science and organisational studies that might help to address these questions. Chapter 5 discusses arts, health and well-being in relation to recent developments in social movement theory, suggesting that this kind of thinking can offer new insights into questions about sustainability and the future development of the field. Chapter 6 explores the related area of boundary work, examining the role of artists in health and care contexts as boundary spanners. This chapter discusses artistic objects as boundary objects and suggests that effective boundary work in arts, health and well-being has the potential to transform and improve many health and care contexts.

References

1. Jones, M. & Daykin, N., Sociology and health, in *Health studies: An introduction*, J. Willis & J. Naidoo (eds). 2015, London: Palgrave. p. 155–171.
2. Stacey, M., *The sociology of health and healing.* 1988, London: Unwin Hyman.
3. Leppert, R., *The sight of sound. Music, representation and the history of the body.* 1993, Berkeley, CA: University of California Press.
4. Daykin, N., *The role of music in arts-based qualitative inquiry.* International Journal of Qualitative Methods, 2004. **3**(2): p. 36–44.
5. Daykin, N., Knowing through music: Implications for research, in *Knowing differently: Arts-based and collaborative research methods*, P. Liamputtong & J. Rumbold (eds). 2008, London: Marion Boyars. p. 229–243.
6. Gabe, J., Kelleher, D. & Williams, G. (eds), *Challenging medicine.* 1994, London: Routledge.
7. Illich, I., *Limits to medicine. Medical nemesis: The expropriation of health.* 1974, London: Marion Boyars.

8. McKeown, T., *The role of medicine: Dream, mirage or nemesis?* 1976, Princeton, NJ: Princeton University Press.

9. McGovern, L., Miller, G. & Hughes-Cromwick P. *Health policy brief: The relative contribution of multiple determinants to health outcomes.* Health Affairs, 2014. http//:healthaffairs.org

10. Arnold, S., Coote, A., Harrison, T., Scurrah, E. & Stephens, L., *Health as a social movement: Theory into practice, programme report.* 2018, London: New Economics Foundation/Royal Society of Arts. https://www.thersa.org/globalassets/hasm-final-report.pdf

11. White, M., *A social tonic: The development of arts in community health.* 2009, Oxford: Radcliffe.

12. Williams, A., *Constructing musicology.* 2001, Aldershot: Ashgate.

13. Boyce-Tillman, J., *Constructing musical healing: The wounds that sing.* 2000, London: Jessica Kingsley Publishers.

14. Daykin, N., *Disruption, dissonance and embodiment: Creativity, health and risk in music narratives.* Health, 2005. **9**(1): p. 67–87.

2 The international field of arts, health and well-being

Introduction

The international field of arts, health and well-being encompasses research, policy and practice on many art forms including music, visual arts, dance, drama and creative writing. These activities take place in diverse settings, including hospitals, care homes, doctors' surgeries, mental health settings, schools, prisons, communities and increasingly in museums, galleries and libraries. They engage diverse populations across the life course, including healthy populations as well as those with diagnosed health conditions. The field is not a unified entity but comprises clusters of activities, networks and resources that have developed in different contexts over many years. Nevertheless, it has grown in visibility over the last 15 years, supported by the research, networking, advocacy and leadership activities of a wide range of stakeholders. As an academic field, it has been underpinned by a growing evidence base and by the development of specialist resources, such as the *Journal of Arts and Health*, which publishes research evidence as well as reviews of policy and practice developments in several countries, including England [1], the USA [2], Canada [3], Australia [4], Denmark [5], Norway and Sweden [6]. Recent issues of the journal indicate the vast range of contexts in which activities such as painting, drawing, photography, music making, signing, crafts, museum and gallery visits and arts therapies are currently used. Research studies of these activities range from improvements in symptoms in people with diagnosed health conditions such as Parkinson's, stroke, chronic obstructive pulmonary disease (COPD) and cancer and changes in physiological markers such as blood pressure and stress to general improvements in health and mental well-being and improvements in clinical practice and quality of care. The arts also contribute to increased public awareness of physical and mental health issues, encouraging inclusive policy dialogue and empowerment in public health.

This chapter discusses the development of the international field of arts, health and well-being. It does not seek to provide a comprehensive overview, as there are some excellent resources available that have mapped the various domains of arts and health [7–10]. Rather, this chapter offers a critical perspective on key issues affecting research, policy and practice, beginning with a discussion of current challenges and their basis in historical and more recent developments.

The development of the international field of arts, health and well-being

The idea that arts and the aesthetic qualities of healing environments are important for health and well-being is not new [1,11]. Horden discusses that the history of music in healthcare has an extensive history, which has been traced back to ancient shamanic practices of creative expression and catharsis that long preceded the development of Western medicine. It is sometimes suggested that prior to the advent of scientific medicine, music and arts held a prominent place within more pluralistic healthcare systems. Up until the mid-18th century, Europeans studying for degrees in medicine would be more exposed to liberal arts education than is currently the case, although historical evidence of the direct therapeutic use of music and arts in healthcare is mixed, and it is difficult to gain an accurate picture of the historical connections between arts and health [12].

The more recent use of art therapies in healthcare in Western Europe has been discussed by Diane Waller, who traces to the increased use of palliative care in military hospitals and factories during the First World War and the growth of psychiatry during the 1920s and 1930s. Interest by early 20th-century doctors in the use of arts in clinical practice, such as the use of patients' drawings for diagnostic purposes, together with the growth of psychiatry as a discipline, created opportunities for artists, whose careers were generally precarious and insecure. These opportunities were reinforced by emerging institutional contexts such as the UK National Health Service, which ended the system of patronage under which artists had previously been engaged, and created formal career structures and parity with other professions allied to medicine [13]. In the UK, art therapists (including art, music, and drama therapists) are registered by the Health and Care Professions Council. Similarly, in the US, art therapy is a protected professional title. However, in international research, the term 'art therapy' is used to describe a wide range of creative practice. In our review of evidence for music and singing interventions for adults, commissioned by the What Works Centre for Wellbeing and led by Professor Christina Victor, we found that the term 'music therapy' is often used to describe a broad range of provision, with no distinction made between services offered by certified and non-certified music therapists [14].

Attempts have been made to map the similarities and differences between art therapies and arts for health and well-being, in what has been characterised as a continuum of practice [15]. Bruschia distinguishes between music *in* therapy and music *as* therapy to differentiate these forms of practice [16]. However, activities such as music in healthcare environments can be delivered by a range of people including arts and music therapists, musicians, nurses, occupational therapists, care staff and volunteers [17]. Activities such as music for dementia patients in a hospital setting could equally be provided by a music therapist or a community musician, while many music therapists work as community musicians alongside their clinical roles. New forms of practice such as community music therapy have further reduced professional distinctions [18,19]. Similarly, art therapists work in a wide variety of health and community settings, offering both one-to-one as well as group-based activities primarily designed to meet a range of goals [20]. It may make more sense to characterise arts interventions in terms of their aims, outcomes, populations and settings rather than simply by the designation of the practitioner offering them.

Underlying challenges: professionalisation, social relations and the role of 'art' in health and well-being

The development of art therapies has influenced the framing of the broader field of arts, health and well-being in several ways. Waller's account discusses some of the key tensions that originated within the art therapy professions and that have a continued impact on the field arts, health and well-being [13]. A commonly reported challenge is that of integrating arts-based approaches within institutional contexts of health and medicine. Despite the expansion of professional opportunities for artists in healthcare, many early art therapists were ambivalent about being drawn into medical organisations, fearing a loss of autonomy and control over their work. The role of medical hierarchies and the effects of disciplinary boundaries continue to be debated within the field of arts, health and well-being.

A second challenge relates to the impact of social relations and inequalities on debates about aesthetics and value in arts, health and well-being. Horden's account of the development of music therapy reveals the way in which specialised practice has been shaped by historical class and gender relations. The early arts therapy professions drew their members from well-educated women and men, and relations of social class and gender shaped their professional identities and their views about art. Hence, early music therapy practitioners tended to favour the therapeutic value of Western 'art music' over other more popular forms such as jazz, which gave rise to moral panics about their corrupting influence [12]. Nowadays, there is much more awareness of the need to challenge social inequalities, and arts are often advocated for purposes of empowerment. However, the effects of social hierarchies can still be seen, for example, in discussions about the nature of artistic quality that sometimes reflect negative views about 'instrumental art', as well as in moral panics about the impact of music genres such as hip hop and rap, or the respective benefits of digital versus live music [21].

Another question surrounds the place of artistic versus clinical values in arts, health and well-being. The pioneers of art therapy were divided between a focus on artistic methods and outcomes and an interest in psychotherapeutic processes involving the unconscious [13]. The dominance of the latter is evident in the British Association of Art Therapy (BAAT) definition of art therapy as a form of psychotherapy that uses art media as its primary mode of expression and communication.[1] Likewise, the American Art Therapy Association describes art therapy as a mental health and human service profession that works by using art making within psychotherapeutic relationships.[2] However, as we have discussed, many arts therapists place more emphasis on artistic values and seek to resist what they see as processes of medicalisation, adopting social models and practices that have much in common with broader arts and health and community arts practice.

These debates often emerge in discussions about definitions of artistic quality in arts for health and well-being as well as debates about the type and level of training, regulation and support that artists in healthcare should receive. An increasing number of education and continuing professional development programmes are available, ranging from project-based supervision and mentoring to accredited modules and courses at universities. However, there is no coordinated leadership of these developments and no agreement about the format, content or level of support that should be provided. On the one hand, it is widely recognised that education and training are essential to enable artists to work safely and effectively with vulnerable people in complex, unfamiliar and often hierarchical environments. Further, education and training in areas such as evaluation as well as project management, fundraising and marketing are important in ensuring the sustainability of projects. On the other hand, there is a reluctance to push artists too far down the route of professionalisation, with fears that this will stifle creativity, increase costs and foster medicalised approaches.

The arts and global health challenges

While internal tensions and challenges have shaped arts, health and well-being as a field, the growth of the field has gained impetus from external forces and from polices that increasingly emphasise asset-based approaches to health and care. External forces are discussed by Clift and Camic in their recent text: they include demographic trends and social challenges that affect most countries in the world. For example, increased life expectancy has been accompanied by growing numbers of people living with chronic mental and physical health conditions, while many societies face new public health challenges of obesity, substance dependence and widening inequalities [22]. These challenges place increasing pressure on services at times when many countries are facing economic crises and policies of austerity. Medicine can offer only limited solutions to these problems, which often stem from social, not medical, causes. It is estimated that up to a fifth of patients consult their GP for what is primarily a social problem [23,24]. Creative arts are often viewed as offering accessible, popular and relatively low-cost solutions within emerging policy agendas.

Responses to demographic and social challenges vary in different cultural contexts. Arts, health and well-being is a global field, increasingly connected by a series of international conferences, networks and social actions. However, its development has been uneven. Clift and Camic document examples of arts for health initiatives in many countries including India, China, Uganda, Brazil, Peru and Venezuela, although they acknowledge that the field of arts, health and well-being has been most strongly recognisable in affluent English-speaking countries [22]. The Nordic and Scandinavian countries have also embraced the use of arts and culture for health [5,6,25,26], although language issues may have contributed to the fact that models developed in countries such as Finland, Sweden and Denmark are less well known than those from the UK, the US, Australia and Canada.

The uneven development of arts, health and well-being as a field may reflect the fact that the power of arts to improve well-being and quality of life is more relevant once basic physical, emotional and social needs are met [22]. However, there has been a long history of artistic expression at the heart of resistance to oppression, with examples ranging from the Mexicanidad Movement of the 1930s featuring artists such as Diego Rivera and Frida Kahlo, the underground jazz scene in Nazi Germany and the oppositional role of rap and hip hop in African American popular culture during the 1990s. While arts on their own cannot address global inequalities, they can help to tackle the social and economic determinants of health [27,28]. Their use extends beyond clinical treatment to include campaigning and advocacy, community social action and education to challenge cultures of poverty and discrimination.

Policy and practice challenges

The uneven development of arts, health and well-being as a field may also reflect cultural differences, including differences in professional roles and resources of institutions, networks and social actors in countries that have actively supported developments. An example of a country where policy makers have explicitly recognised the role of arts is Finland. The Finnish government has espoused a long-term objective to make arts-based and culture-based well-being services a permanent part of health and care services. Policies include a percentage for art operating model, which means that a percentage of the budget for capital construction projects in health is protected for the arts. The Finnish Government has supported the coordination centre, Taikusydän,[3] which works across the field of arts, culture and well-being to support research and practice developments, as well as the ArtsEqual research initiative, coordinated by the University of the Arts Helsinki, which examines the arts as public service and explores how they can meet the social challenges of the 2020s.[4]

In many countries, support for arts in health and care has been fragmented and piecemeal. For example, in the UK, policies affecting arts, health and well-being are shaped by several agencies and public bodies, and support for the field from policy leaders has been inconsistent. The field has often drawn its energy from the efforts of grass-roots activists and networks, some of which came together recently to form the Culture, Health and Wellbeing Alliance, supported by Arts Council England. More recently, policies such as decentralisation and devolving commissioning of health services to local providers have created opportunities for arts. For example, the Cultural Commissioning Programme (CCP) was funded by ACE and led by the National Council for Voluntary Organisations (NCVO) between 2013 and 2017. This programme brought together arts and cultural organisations with public service commissioners to help them explore creative ways of working to deliver improved outcomes, particularly in the areas of mental health and well-being, older people and place-based commissioning [29].

While the uneven development of arts, health and well-being reflects different cultural contexts and policy environments, there has been some convergence of practice, with models such as social prescribing being adopted in several countries. Social prescribing is an example of an asset-based approach to addressing health and well-being which involves identifying strengths and potentials within communities and mobilising members to take appropriate action to address local needs [30]. Social prescribing enables referral of people with health and well-being needs to local, non-clinical services, including arts and cultural activities. In the UK, social prescribing is linked with personalised care and is seen as a means of reducing the pressure on services [31–33]. Social prescribing has also been used in the Scandinavian countries, for example, the Swedish Government has sponsored initiatives such as the Culture and Health Association as well as more focused initiatives around older people, chronic conditions and mental health [34].

Emerging models such as social prescribing have given impetus to the arts and health sector, but several challenges as well as prerequisites for successful asset-based approaches have been identified [30–32; 35–37]. These reports document ongoing challenges including questions about funding and the struggle to manage rising demand for services as well competing priorities within reduced budgets. There are issues of capacity, with the arts and health sector often made up of small, fragmented organisations, or even sole practitioners, which can make it difficult for individuals and professionals to access appropriate services. There have also been calls for a stronger evidence base, since research on the impact of programmes such as social prescribing is in its early stages, with a preponderance of small-scale evaluations and no consensus about the type or level of evidence required to justify support for arts in health and care. Prerequisites for successful social prescribing and other asset-based approaches to health and care have been identified including communication and 'buy in' from a complex web of stakeholders, the use of skilled link workers who can establish and maintain relationships between partners, the capacity of leaders to listen to local people and respond to their interests, early intervention to prevent problems from developing and a shift towards cultures of power sharing between health and social care staff and service users.

Case study: the Creative and Credible project

Experiences of using arts-based assets to address local health and care needs were explored in our Creative and Credible study of stakeholder views and experiences of co-production in arts, health and well-being.[5] The project brought together a Stakeholder Reference Group comprising artists, health professionals, commissioners, funders and researchers, who had experience of developing and evaluating arts-based approaches across a wide variety of contexts. The group met regularly over a one-year period to discuss current challenges, including evaluation issues and methodologies in arts, health and well-being. An online survey as well as interviews and focus groups documented stakeholders' experiences, finding many examples of successful co-production and of arts being used effectively to address local needs. Stakeholders reported using a wide range of evaluation tools, but they also reported difficulties in evaluation practice and practice development. These often seemed to arise from mismatched, unclear or unrealistic expectations of what the arts can deliver, as well as language and cultural differences across different sectors and professional groups [38].

A key finding was that artists can often feel disadvantaged in exchanges led by health and medical professionals, particularly in discussions about evaluation. There was a perception that arts-based perspectives held little traction in debates with commissioners and funders, who tended to favour notions of a hierarchy of evidence drawn from evidence-based medicine. This sometimes led to the adoption of evaluation methods and tools that did not suit the stage of development of small projects and failed to adequately reflect the experiences, needs and priorities of project participants.

Hierarchies of evidence rank experimental methods such as randomised control trials (RCTs) more highly than other methods, with low ranked 'anecdotal' approaches viewed as lacking in validity. RCTs compare data from project participants with non-participants before and after interventions, with participants randomly allocated to intervention or control group. The design of RCTs is intended to identify intervention outcomes and separate the effects of participation from other factors that might influence these outcomes. Randomised trials, and meta-analysis of data from trails, are generally accepted within healthcare as the highest forms of evidence on which to base healthcare interventions.[6] However, challenges of evaluating complex arts activities and programmes with subtle and wide-ranging outcomes using this framework are frequently acknowledged. Difficulties include recruiting sufficient numbers of participants to studies, applying randomisation procedures to research and 'blinding' arts engagement [39]. While hierarchies of evidence are accepted within healthcare, they are viewed with ambivalence within the arts and cultural sector, where other forms of evidence, such as qualitative research, case studies and unpublished 'grey' literature, are valued more highly [40]. For example, the Creative and Credible stakeholders were aware of the benefits that creative approaches could bring not just to health and well-being but also to evaluation processes themselves. There were enthusiastic discussions about the use of evaluation methods using photography, film, visual arts and music, which were advocated as providing valuable new insights and perspectives as well as empowering participants and enriching dissemination. Nevertheless, few stakeholders reported using such methods in practice, as they assumed (sometimes incorrectly) that commissioners and funders would find them unconvincing.

These findings reflect a common perception of the difficulty of making artistic world views count in a field that is dominated by medical and scientific discourse. This can lead to frustration and a perception that arts experiences may be diminished in order to fit within existing healthcare performance indicators and data monitoring systems. It can lead to a sense of inequality that can undermine processes of co-production and can render evaluation a burden to artists, project participants and other stakeholders. The Creative and Credible study revealed that co-production requires all partners to be on a relatively equal footing from the start, and that time needs to be taken in order to enable actors to appreciate each other's standpoints and develop a shared vision and language. However, this is difficult to achieve in practice, not helped by the fact that the arts and health sector is often fragmented, with small organisations facing increasing competition for diminishing resources and struggling to find an equal voice in negotiations with policy makers and funders. This suggests the need for capacity building to support bottom-up as well as top-down approaches to arts, health and well-being, as well as policy agendas that seek to address a broad range of health and social needs.

In order to help to address these challenges, the Creative and Credible project developed a free online knowledge base designed to support evaluation of arts programmes in health and well-being (http://creativeandcredible.co.uk/). In collaboration with the Royal Society of Public Health, the team continues to offer regular training events for artists, programme managers, commissioners, funders and policy makers.

Conclusions

This chapter has reviewed the development of the international field of arts, health and well-being. Despite uneven development and variations in policy approaches in different countries, there has been some convergence towards recognising the role of arts within asset-based approaches to health, such as social prescribing. Several challenges remain, including funding and resources, the role of evidence, difficulties in communication and collaborative working and issues of power sharing between stakeholders. While the field has often drawn its energy from the efforts of grass-roots activists, practitioners and networks, these groups have been disproportionately affected by funding constraints and the impact of austerity-driven policies. There is a need to build capacity at the grass-roots level in order to strengthen practice, reduce inequalities and enable multiple voices to influence the development of innovative responses to contemporary health and social care challenges.

Notes

1 https://www.baat.org/About-Art-Therapy
2 https://arttherapy.org/about-art-therapy/
3 https://taikusydan.turkuamk.fi/
4 http://www.artsequal.fi/
5 The Creative and Credible project is a partnership among the University of the West of England, Bristol, Willis Newson arts consultants, the University of Winchester and the Royal Society of Public Health. The initial research was funded by the Economic and Social Research Council.
6 The Oxford Centre for Evidence-Based Medicine produces information and guidance on many aspects of evidence-based medicine, including levels of evidence (https://www.cebm.net/).

References

1. Clift, S., Camic, P, Chapman, B., Clayton, G., Daykin, N., Eades, G., Parkinson, C., Secker, J., Stickley, T. & White, M., *The state of arts and health in England*. Arts and Health: An International Journal of Research, Policy and Practice, 2009. **1**(1): p. 6–35.
2. Sonke, J., Rollins, J., Brandman, R. & Graham-Pole, J., *The state of arts in healthcare in the United States*. Arts and Health: An International Journal of Research, Policy and Practice, 2009. **1**(2): p. 107–135.
3. Cox, S. M., Lafrenière, D., Brett-MacLean, P., Collie, K., Cooley, N., Dunbrack, J. & Frager, G, *Tipping the iceberg? The state of arts and health in Canada*. Arts and Health: An International Journal of Research, Policy and Practice, 2010. **2**(2): p. 109–124.

4. Wreford, G., *The state of arts and health in Australia.* Arts and Health: An International Journal of Research, Policy and Practice, 2010. **2**(1): p. 8–22.
5. Jensen, A., *Beyond the borders: the use of art participation for the promotion of health and well-being in Britain and Denmark.* Arts and Health: An International Journal of Research, Policy and Practice, 2013. **5**(3): p. 204–215.
6. Cuypers, K. F., Knudtsen, M. S., Sandgren, M., Krokstad, S., Wikström, B. M. & Theorell, T., *Cultural activities and public health: research in Norway and Sweden. An overview.* Arts and Health: An International Journal of Research, Policy and Practice, 2011. **3**(1): p. 6–26.
7. Fancourt, D., *Arts in health. Designing and researching interventions.* 2017, Oxford: Oxford University Press.
8. Clift, S. & Camic, P. M., *Oxford textbook of creative arts, health, and well-being.* 2016, Oxford: Oxford University Press.
9. All Party Parliamentary Group on Arts, Health and Wellbeing, *Creative health: The arts for health and wellbeing.* 2017, London: APPG. www.arts healthandwellbeing.org.uk/appg/inquiry
10. Arts Council England, *Arts and culture in health and wellbeing and in the criminal justice system. A summary of the evidence.* 2018, London: ACE. https://www.artscouncil.org.uk/publication/arts-and-culture-health-and-wellbeing-and-criminal-justice-system-summary-evidence
11. Belfiore, E., The arts and healing: The power of an idea, in *Oxford textbook of creative arts, health, and wellbeing*, S. Clift & P.M. Camic (eds). 2016, Oxford: Oxford University Press. p. 11–17.
12. Horden, P., *Music as medicine. The history of music therapy since antiquity.* 2000, London: Routledge.
13. Waller, D., *Becoming a profession: The history of art therapy in Britain 1940–1982.* 1991, London and New York: Routledge.
14. Daykin, N., Mansfield, L., Meads, C., Julier, G., Tomlinson, A., Payne, A., Grigsby Duffy, L., Lane, J., D'Innocenzo, G., Burnett, A., Kay, T., Dolan, P., Testoni, S. & Victor, C., *What works for wellbeing? A systematic review of wellbeing outcomes for music and singing in adults.* Perspect Public Health, 2018. **138**(1): p. 39–46.
15. Daykin, N. & Bunt. L., Music as a resource for health and wellbeing, in *International handbook of occupational therapy interventions*, I. Söderback (ed). 2015, Cham: Springer. p. 453–456.
16. Bruscia, K., *Defining music therapy* (2nd ed.). 1998, Gilsum, NH: Barcelona Publications.
17. Daykin, N., Bunt, L. & McLean, S., *Music and healing in cancer care: A survey of supportive care providers.* The Arts in Psychotherapy, 2006. **33**: p. 402–413.
18. Ansdell, G. *How music helps in music therapy and everyday life.* 2014. Farnham: Asgate.
19. Pavlicevic, M. & Ansdell, G., *Community music therapy.* 2004, London and Philadelphia, PA: Jessica Kingsley Publishers.

20. Hogan, S., *Healing arts. The history of art therapy.* 2001, London: Jessica Kingsley Publishers.
21. Daykin, N., de Viggiani, N., Pilkington, P. & Moriarty, Y., *Music-making for health and wellbeing in youth justice settings: Mediated affordances and the impact of context and social relations.* Sociology of Health and Illness, 2013. **39**(6): p. 941–958.
22. Clift, S. & Camic, P.M., Introduction to the field of creative arts, wellbeing and health: Achievements and current challenges, in *Oxford textbook of creative arts, health, and wellbeing. International perspectives on practice, policy, and research*, S. Clift & P. M. Camic (ed). 2016, Oxford: Oxford University Press. p. 3–10.
23. Torjesen, I., *Social prescribing could help alleviate pressure on GPs.* BMJ, 2016. **352**: p. i1436.
24. The Low Commission, *The role of advice services in health outcomes: Evidence review and mapping study.* 2015, The Low Commission. www.lowcommission.org.uk/dyn/1435582011755/ASA-report
25. Theorell, T., Knudtsen, M. S., Horwitz, E. B. & Wikström, B. M., Culture and public health activities in Sweden and Norway, in *Oxford textbook of creative arts, health and wellbeing: International perspectives on practice, policy and research*, S. Clift & P. M. Camic (eds). 2015, Oxford: Oxford University Press. p. 171–177.
26. Jensen, A., Stickley, T., Torrissen, W. & Stigmar, K., *Arts on prescription in Scandinavia: A review of current practice and future possibilities.* Perspectives in Public Health, 2017. **137**(5): p. 268–274.
27. Marmot, M., *Fair society, healthy lives: The Marmot Review: Strategic review of health inequalities in England post-2010.* 2010, London: The Marmot Review. www.ucl.ac.uk/marmotreview
28. Clift, S., Camic, P. M. & Daykin, N., *The arts and global health inequalities.* Arts and Health: An International Journal of Research, Policy and Practice, 2010. **2**: p. 3–7.
29. Parkinson, A. & Wilkie, S., *Evaluation of the cultural commissioning programme: Final Report.* 2016, Consilium Research and Consultancy/National Council for Voluntary Organisations. https://www.ncvo.org.uk/images/documents/practical_support/public_services/cultural-commissioning/cultural-commissioning-programme-evaluation-may-2016.pdf
30. Polley, M., Fleming, J., Anfilogoff, T. & Carpenter, A., *Making sense of social prescribing.* 2017. London: University of Westminster. https://westminsterresearch.westminster.ac.uk/item/q1v77/making-sense-of-social-prescribing.
31. Kings Fund, *What is social prescribing?* 2017, London: The Kings Fund. https://www.kingsfund.org.uk/publications/social-prescribing
32. Chatterjee, H. J., Camic, P. M., Lockyer, B. & Thomson, L. J. M., *Non-clinical community interventions: A systematised review of social prescribing schemes.* Arts & Health, 2018. **10**(2): p. 97–123.

33. NHS England, *Social prescribing and community-based support. Summary guide.* 2019, London. https://www.england.nhs.uk/wp-content/uploads/2019/01/social-prescribing-community-based-support-summary-guide.pdf

34. Jensen, A., Stickley, T., Torrissen, W. & Stigmar, K., *Arts on prescription in Scandinavia: A review of current practice and future possibilities.* Perspectives in Public Health, 2017. **137**(5): p. 268–274.

35. Arnold, S., Coote, A., Harrison, T., Scurrah, E. & Stephens, L., *Health as a social movement: Theory into practice, programme report.* 2018, London: New Economics Foundation/Royal Society of Arts. https://www.thersa.org/globalassets/hasm-final-report.pdf

36. Bickerdike, L., Booth, A., Wilson, P. M., Farley, K. & Wright, K., *Social prescribing: Less rhetoric and more reality. A systematic review of the evidence.* BMJ Open, 2017. doi:10.1136/bmjopen-2016–013384

37. Polley, M., Bertotti, M., Kimberlee, R., Pilkington, K. & Refsum, C. *A review of the evidence assessing impact of social prescribing on healthcare demand and cost implications.* 2017, London: University of Westminster.

38. Daykin, N., Willis, J., McCree, M. & Gray, K., *Creative and credible evaluation for arts, health and wellbeing: Opportunities and challenges of coproduction.* Arts and Health: An International Journal of Research, Policy and Practice, 2016. **9**(2): p. 123–138.

39. Clift, S., Camic, P., Chapman, B., Clayton, G., Daykin, N., Eades, G., Parkinson, C., Secker, J., Stickley, T. & White, M., *The state of arts and health in England.* Arts and Health: An International Journal of Research, Policy and Practice, 2009. **1**(1): p. 6–35.

40. Daykin, N., Mansfield, L., Payne, A., Kay, T., Meads, C., D'Innocenzo, G., Burnett, A., Dolan, P., Julier, G., Longworth, L., Tomlinson, A., Testoni, S. & Victor, C., *What works for wellbeing in culture and sport? Report of a DELPHI process to support coproduction and establish principles and parameters of an evidence review.* Perspect Public Health, 2017. **137**(5): p. 281–288.

3 Research and evidence in arts, health and well-being

Introduction

This chapter presents a brief overview of research findings and evidence in arts, health and well-being. As the field has expanded, the evidence base has also grown, and recent years have seen a burgeoning of research on the impacts of creative arts health and community settings, supported by specialist journals, websites and research repositories. Participation in arts and culture has been associated with a wide range of outcomes and impacts, from improvements in individual health and well-being to enhanced community cohesion and reduced social exclusion [1–4]. However, as the field expands, it is increasingly difficult to map or summarise the evidence across the entire range of arts and cultural interventions and activities.

In her recent book, Daisy Fancourt identifies seven domains of arts and health research that might be viewed as sub-fields for the purposes of future evidence reviews [5]. These domains include targeted interventions, including participatory arts and arts to enhance health-care environments such as hospitals GP surgeries, hospices and care homes; arts therapies; arts on prescription and social prescribing; arts in healthcare technology; arts-based public health and health promotion; broader cultural engagement such as singing in a choir, learning an instrument, dancing or visiting museums and galleries; and the use of arts in the education of healthcare professionals and the public. To date, the bulk of research has focused on targeted participatory arts, spanning a wide range of art forms including visual arts, music, drama, creative writing and dance. Participatory arts include open access activities, such as singing in a well-being choir, as well as activities that are targeted at people with identified conditions such as mental health conditions, cancer, chronic obstructive pulmonary disease (COPD), Parkinson's disease and dementia. Research on participatory arts also encompasses projects with 'at risk' populations in schools, hospitals, mental healthcare, justice settings, public health and community settings.

Mapping the evidence base for arts, health and well-being

Early reviews of evidence on arts, health and well-being focused on the clinical effects of arts interventions, particularly music, in healthcare settings. The review by Rosalia Staricoff, commissioned by Arts Council England, examined 385 controlled studies of performing and creative arts in healthcare published between 1990 and 2004 [6]. The review cited positive effects of arts in cancer care, cardiovascular care, neonatal intensive care, surgery and mental health. Arts were linked with a range of outcomes including reduced anxiety and depression, improved pain management, effects on vital signs such as blood pressure, reduced need for medication and reduced length of stay in hospital. The review also found evidence for arts- and humanities-based education and training in enhancing the observational skills and empathy of clinicians. The report identified gaps in the literature, including a need to understand the contribution of different art forms to health outcomes and a lack of rigorous research on the broader social and community impacts of arts activities.

The Staricoff review was updated in 2011 by Staricoff and Clift in a report that identified 103 studies of the effects of music interventions in hospital care [7]. The report identified positive psychological and physiological outcomes discussed under the headings of maternity, neonatal and intensive care, children, cardiovascular conditions, surgery and pain management, lung diseases and oncology. A follow-up review in 2014 reported a range of benefits and challenges of music and arts in healthcare environments [8,9]. Music listening was reported to affect physiological signs such as blood pressure, heart rate and respiratory rates, as well as helping to reduce stress and anxiety and increasing patients' ability to cope and their sense of control. However, the report notes some challenges, including the fact that music listening interventions in healthcare environments are sometimes undertaken without consideration for patient or service user choice or preference in relation to the type or style of music. The review included studies of other art forms including dancing, singing and drawing, reporting positive impacts of these, including increased patient satisfaction, reduced length of stay in hospital, cost benefits as well as enjoyment, appreciation of cultural traditions and opportunities for social interaction and connection with others. Participatory arts in healthcare settings were also found to contribute to improved staff well-being and reduced stress, although healthcare staff sometimes report feelings of embarrassment when invited to take part in activities such as music making [8,9].

As well as these broad reviews, an increasing number of focused evidence reviews have been undertaken in specific topic areas. Findings from these reviews suggest that arts interventions can be effective in enhancing health and well-being, addressing many challenges across the life course. Recent findings include the following:

- In children and young people, performing arts such as drama and music have been shown to have positive effects on peer interaction, social skills, mood and health knowledge [10] while dance-based activities may improve physical and psychosocial well-being [11,12].
- For young people from disadvantaged population groups and those considered at risk, music making has been associated with a range of outcomes including reduced anxiety and depression, improved school attendance, personal empowerment and healthy nutrition [13].
- Music in youth justice settings can improve young people's confidence, self-esteem and mood [14].
- In healthy adult populations, music has been shown to contribute to enhanced mood and purpose, while for those with diagnosed health conditions, there is evidence for efficacy in relation to enhanced mental well-being, quality of life, self-awareness and coping [15].
- Arts have been found to have positive effects on mental healthcare environments, promoting recovery in adults with mental health conditions and improving wayfinding in dementia care. However, arts interventions do not necessarily address the lack of control exercised by patients in mental healthcare environments [16,17].
- In older people, research has identified physical effects of activities such as dance such as improvements in muscular strength and endurance, balance and fitness [18]. Participatory arts have also been found to contribute to improvements in cardiovascular function, joint mobility and breathing and can improve confidence and self-esteem in this group [19]. Music and singing have been shown to be effective in enhancing morale and reducing risk of depression in older people [15].
- Arts-based interventions in education and training of health professionals can contribute to enhanced well-being of staff and reduced risk of errors, enhanced teamwork and improved diagnostic observation skills in medical practitioners [20,21].

This overview of findings from evidence reviews is by no means intended as comprehensive, rather, it indicates the range and breadth of evidence regarding health and well-being outcomes of targeted art forms with different populations across the life course and in a wide variety of settings. The reviews suggest that creative and performing arts can contribute to a wide range of health and well-being outcomes. They also reflect a general trend towards the use of more robust research approaches, including the increasing use of randomised control trials and experimental designs. Nevertheless, it can be challenging to apply such methodologies in arts, health and well-being. Robust studies often require relatively large samples, whereas many arts and health projects are small and relatively short lived. Several methodological limitations continue to affect the evidence base, including issues of sampling and selection bias, lack of comparators and a focus on positive outcomes and impacts [1]. Qualitative research can provide insights into participants' experiences of arts and the factors that affect project delivery, including issues of power and control, perceptions and influence of key stakeholders and the extent of user participation. However, qualitative research can be time-consuming and resource intensive, and it is not a useful vehicle for providing reliable data on project outcomes.

As well as examining the effects of targeted arts interventions, a growing body of research, including several large-scale longitudinal studies in the Nordic countries, has explored the impact of general arts and cultural participation on health and well-being. Fifteen studies were reviewed by Gordon-Nesbitt [22], who reported that cultural participation has been positively associated with survival rates, as well as physical health and subjective well-being. More recently, museum attendance has been linked with benefits for older adults including reductions in cognitive decline, reduced dementia and reduced depression [23–25].

Researching the impact of general cultural participation on health and well-being involves similar methodological difficulties to those found in evaluation of interventions, with the additional challenge that visiting museums, attending concerts and other recreational activities are deeply woven into everyday life [26]. While large-scale and longitudinal surveys have provided evidence of associations between cultural participation and health, it can be challenging to establish cause and effect relationships in these studies [27]. The data may reflect the fact that those who participate may already have better health than those who do not engage, since those who enjoy good health are more likely and able to participate. Hence, participation may be a consequence rather than a cause of good health and well-being, and health differences might arise from other factors such as income and education level. Research can to some extent take into account the fact that culturally active and engaged people may differ from those who are inactive or not engaged, for example, by using statistical techniques to control for confounding variables such as education level, income, pre-existing health conditions, disability and lifestyle factors such as smoking and physical activity. Several studies have suggested that effects of cultural participation on mortality and morbidity are maintained after controlling for socioeconomic variables, indicating that arts and cultural participation may have an independent effect on health and well-being [23–25, 28]. This suggests that targeted arts and cultural activities and programmes can contribute to reducing health and well-being inequalities.

Most of the research in the burgeoning arts and health field examines the effects of participation or engagement on individuals. Fewer studies have documented the wider social benefits of community-based arts projects and activities. Assessing the social impacts of arts and culture can be difficult for several reasons. There is no common usage of terms such as 'impact' and 'community', which can be defined in many ways, and it is difficult to pinpoint community impacts, since most outcome measures focus on individuals [29]. An early review by Matarasso (1997) surveyed 513 participants in 60 projects, identifying themes of personal development, social cohesion, community empowerment, local image and identity, imagination and vision, and health and well-being in relation to participatory arts [30]. More recently, a review of participatory arts and older people reported evidence that arts can offer opportunities for meaningful social contact, friendship and support. The authors report that participation enabled people to feel that they were contributing to society and enhanced relationships between participants and carers as well as transforming public attitudes by challenging negative perceptions of older people and reducing stigma [19].

Studies of arts and community well-being have tended to focus on notions of social capital, focusing on a variety of impacts of participatory arts beyond encouraging individual creativity, skills development and well-being. Participatory arts are seen as contributing to social capital by connecting people, supporting neighbourhood improvement, fostering cultural cohesion, engendering collective pride and efficacy, promoting learning and extending the capacity of organisations [29]. Social capital theorists often draw on Putnam's work to identify benefits of social connection [31,32]. A smaller number of researchers have followed Bourdieu [33] to drawn attention to the negative effects of social and cultural capital. Ideas surrounding arts, such as judgement and taste, have often been used to reinforce social divisions and preserve the positions of those with higher status and control of resources. These may influence participants' experiences and reports of negative impacts such as anxieties around competency and capability voiced by some participants in performing arts projects [12]. Qualitative researchers have explored the unequal distribution of social capital and the mechanisms and micro-level processes through which inequalities can be reproduced and sustained in community projects, through actions and interactions of participants, professionals and gatekeepers [34].

Those using social capital theory to explore the empowering aspects of arts often distinguish between bonding and bridging social capital. Bonding social capital relates to the nature or relationships within groups, while bridging social capital refers to connections between social groups across divisions of social class, ethnicity, education or other characteristics. While bonding social capital might reinforce supportive connections within communities, this may be detrimental to well-being if it is linked with closure or exclusion of external perspectives and communities. Bridging social capital may be helpful for disadvantaged communities as it is viewed as leading to extended networks, increased access to resources and the development of shared values and trust. Bridging social capital, therefore, has the potential to overcome social divisions and address exclusion [3]. These two forms of capital are not mutually exclusive, however. Arts participation can reinforce group cohesion at the same time as connecting communities in a form of social capital characterised as 'bridged bonding' [35].

Another topic that has begun to feature more strongly in research within the field is that of economic impact and cost-effectiveness. Policy makers have shown interest in the potential cost-savings that can arise from utilising arts and creativity in health and care. The report of the All Party Parliamentary Inquiry into arts health and well-being documents a range of financial benefits including savings in the areas of early years care and education, reduced GP consultation rates, reductions in hospital admissions, reduced agitation and need for medication in people with dementia [4]. Community benefits of culture and sport have also been identified, with one estimate in

2015 suggesting that the value of income gains arising from higher subjective well-being amounts to £1,084 per person per year or £90 per person per month [36].

How to access research and evidence on arts, health and well-being

While the research base for arts, health and well-being is constantly expanding, those outside academic institutions, such as community artists, project leaders, evaluators and commissioners, often face difficulties in obtaining up-to-date research and evidence. Many reports and evaluations relevant to arts, health and well-being do not find their way into the published literature. These reports are classified as 'grey literature' and are often missed by online searches. Even when the evidence can be accessed, identifying and evaluating relevant studies from the vast numbers of published papers available can be a challenging task for busy practitioners and project leaders. Arts practitioners and project leaders who take part in training and networking events such as the Creative and Credible series, discussed in the previous chapter, often report that it is difficult to keep track of the evidence. These problems have sometimes contributed to a lack of awareness of existing practice and attempts to 'reinvent the wheel' when developing new interventions and projects. Fortunately, current trends, such as the move towards open accessing publishing, are making it easier for those outside academic institutions to access evidence. Specialist resources such as the Creative and Credible website (http://creativeand credible.co.uk/) provide guidance on how to conduct a simple evidence review. The remainder of this section gives details of various sources of evidence and where up-to-date information, including unpublished 'grey literature', can be accessed.

Reports of evidence on arts, health and well-being can be found in an increasing number of systematic reviews and evidence reviews. Systematic reviews draw together a wide range of evidence on a specific topic, synthesising quantitative and qualitative findings and assessing the quality of evidence in order to inform policy and practice. Systematic reviews focus on published research, often on arts therapies in clinical settings. They can be found on databases such as the Cochrane library[1] and PROSPERO, which is an international database of prospectively registered systematic reviews with health-related outcomes across health and social care, public health, education, crime, justice and international development.[2]

In the past, systematic reviews have focused on peer review publications and emphasised clinical outcomes of arts. More recently, the What Works Centre for Wellbeing is an evidence review programme that includes quantitative and qualitative research, including grey literature, with a focus on well-being rather than health.[3] Recent review topics include the following:

- Music and singing for adults [15]
- Sport and dance for young people [12]
- Visual arts in mental health [17]
- Outdoor recreation and family well-being [37]
- Heritage and well-being [38]
- Interventions for tackling loneliness in culture and sport [39]

Research on arts and health can also be found in specialist publications, such as *Arts and Health,*[4] the *Journal of Applied Arts and Health*[5] and the recently established *Nordic Journal of Arts and Health.*[6] Another recent initiative, a repository of arts and health grey literature resources, has been created with the support of the Royal Society of Public Health and several other organisations in order to make arts and health research more available to those outside of academia.[7]

Conclusions

The burgeoning research and evidence surrounding arts, health and well-being continues to grow both in terms of quantity and quality. To date, research has focused on clinical and non-clinical outcomes in a variety of contexts; a smaller number of researchers have examined social and economic impacts of participation in arts and culture. There are ongoing research challenges that affect evaluation of many complex health and care interventions, with a need for larger studies with longer term follow-up. Quantitative research challenges are being addressed through improvements in sampling, randomisation, outcome measures and reporting and in the use of advanced techniques to address causality in longitudinal studies. Qualitative research can be improved by more critical use of underlying theoretical frameworks and clearer reporting of methodological issues. Some gaps in the evidence base have been identified. Most studies tend to report benefits of participation. However, participants sometimes report negative experiences, including creative tensions, stress and difficulties with group dynamics. Further attention needs to be paid to the risk and challenges of arts, including negative experiences of individuals and communities, and the factors and forces that shape these, including social hierarchies, power relationships and issues of control.

A key challenge is understanding the potential impact of arts and culture on health and well-being inequalities. It is widely recognised that those who are most actively involved with the arts and culture tend to be from more privileged backgrounds in terms of levels of education, socio-economic background and geographical location than those who engage the least. Participants in arts projects often tend to be female and relatively well educated, and research studies can struggle to recruit participants from disadvantaged and marginalised backgrounds [15]. Yet several longitudinal studies discussed in this chapter have identified an independent effect of arts on health and well-being, suggesting that arts can contribute to reducing inequalities. Further research is needed to examine these effects, including research on the effects of arts participation on inequalities of gender, ethnicity, sexual orientation and disability.

Research issues and findings are explored in relation to selected studies in Chapter 4. These show that, like other complex interventions in health and care, arts can be difficult to evaluate. However, research challenges are unlikely to be resolved by methodology alone, as they reflect underlying policy choices and practice issues. For example, there is unlikely to be a strong consensus about the type and level of evidence that is needed to justify support for the arts. This is because issues of power, status and control over resources often lie behind disagreements about research and evidence. This can be seen in the dominance of clinical perspectives in current research, which focuses on improvements in physical or mental health, adopting hierarchies of evidence in which perspectives from the arts carry relatively little weight. Hence, recent publications, 'rarely examine the artistic motivations and achievements of this kind of work' [1] p. 31.

This suggests that the evidence does not simply speak for itself. In order to understand the relationships and processes that shape and limit arts in health and care, it is necessary to draw on alternative theoretical frameworks to those of evidence-based healthcare. Chapters 5 and 6 consider theories developed in social sciences and organisational studies, including those used in the study of social movements and boundary work, to understand the broader context of arts in health and care and to identify implications for the scope and future development of the field.

Notes

1 https://www.cochranelibrary.com/
2 https://www.crd.york.ac.uk/PROSPERO/
3 https://whatworkswellbeing.org/
4 https://www.tandfonline.com/toc/rahe20/current
5 https://www.intellectbooks.com/journal-of-applied-arts-health
6 https://www.idunn.no/nordic_journal_of_arts_culture_and_health?
   languageId=2
7 http://www.artshealthresources.org.uk/

References

1. Arts Council England, *Arts and culture in health and wellbeing and in the criminal justice system. A summary of the evidence.* 2018, Manchester: ACE. https://www.artscouncil.org.uk/publication/arts-and-culture-health-and-wellbeing-and-criminal-justice-system-summary-evidence

2. Mowlah, A., Niblett, V., Blackburn, J. & Harris, M., *The value of arts and culture to people and society.* 2014, Manchester: Arts Council England. https://www.artscouncil.org.uk/publication/value-arts-and-culture-people-and-society

3. Taylor, P., Davies, L., Wells, P., Gilbertson, J. & Tayleur, W., *A review of the social impacts of culture and sport. CASE: The culture and sport evidence programme.* 2015, London: Department of Culture, Media and Sport. https://assets.publishing.service.gov.uk/government/uploads/system/uploads/attachment_data/file/416279/A_review_of_the_Social_Impacts_of_Culture_and_Sport.pdf.

4. All Party Parliamentary Group on Arts, Health and Wellbeing, *Creative health: The arts for health and wellbeing.* 2017, London: APPG. www.artshealthandwellbeing.org.uk/appg/inquiry

5. Fancourt, D., *Arts in health. Designing and researching interventions.* 2017, Oxford: Oxford University Press.

6. Staricoff, R., *Arts in health: A review of the medical literature.* 2004, London: Arts Council England. www.artscouncil.org.uk/publication_archive/arts-in-health-a-review-of-the-medical-literature

7. Staricoff, R. & Clift., S., *Arts and music in healthcare: An overview of the medical literature: 2004–2011.* 2011, London: Chelsea and Westminster Health Charity, Sidney de Haan Research Centre for Arts and Health, Canterbury Christ Church University.

8. Boyce, M., Bungay, H., Munn-Giddings, C. & Wilson, C., *The impact of the arts in healthcare on patients and service users: A critical review.* Health and Social Care in the Community, 2018. **26**: p. 458–473.

9. Bungay, H., Munn-Giddings, C., Boyce, M. & Wilson, C., *The value of the arts in therapeutic and clinical interventions: A critical review of the literature.* 2014, Anglia Ruskin University. https://arro.anglia.ac.uk/582341/1/The%20Value%20of%20the%20Arts_WEB.pdf

10. Daykin, N., Orme, J., Evans, D., Salmon, D., McEachran, M. & Brain, S., *The impact of participation in performing arts on adolescent health and behaviour: A systematic review of the literature.* Journal of Health Psychology, 2008. **13**(2): p. 251–264.
11. Burkhardt, J. & Brennan, C., *The effects of recreational dance interventions on the health and well-being of children and young people: A systematic review.* Arts & Health, 2012. **4**(2): p. 148–161.
12. Mansfield, L., Kay, T., Meads, C., Grigsby-Duffy, L., Lane, J., John, A., Daykin, N., Dolan, P., Testoni, S., Julier, G., Payne, A., Tomlinson, A. & Victor, C., *Sport and dance interventions for healthy young people (15–24 years) to promote subjective well-being: A systematic review.* BMJ Open, 2018. **8**(7): p. e020959.
13. Cain, M., Lakhani, A. & Istvandity, L., *Short and long term outcomes for culturally and linguistically diverse (CALD) and at-risk communities in participatory music programs: A systematic review.* Arts & Health, 2016. **8**(2): p. 105–124.
14. Daykin, N., de Viggiani, N., Pilkington, P. & Moriarty, Y., *Music making for health, well-being and behaviour change in youth justice settings: A systematic review.* Health Promotion International, 2013. **28**(2): p. 197–210.
15. Daykin, N., Mansfield, L., Meads, C., Julier, G., Tomlinson, A., Payne, A., Grigsby Duffy, L., Lane, J., D'Innocenzo, G., Burnett, A., Kay, T., Dolan, P., Testoni, S. & Victor, C., *What works for wellbeing? A systematic review of wellbeing outcomes for music and singing in adults.* Perspect Public Health, 2018. **138**(1): p. 39–46.
16. Daykin, N., Byrne. E., Soteriou, T. & O'Connor S., *The impact of art, design and environment in mental healthcare: A systematic review of the literature.* Journal of the Royal Society for the Promotion of Health, 2008. **128**(2): p. 85–94.
17. Tomlinson, A., Lane, J., Julier, G., Grigsby Duffy, L., Payne, A., Mansfield, L., Kay, T., John, A., Meads, C., Daykin, N., Ball, K., Tapson, C., Dolan, P., Testoni, S. & Victor, C., *A systematic review of the subjective wellbeing outcomes of engaging with visual arts for adults ('working age', 15–64 years) with diagnosed mental health conditions.* 2018, London: What Works Centre for Wellbeing. https://whatworkswell being.org/product/visual-arts/
18. Hwang, P. W. & Braun, K. L. *The effectiveness of dance interventions to improve older adults' health: A systematic literature review.* Alternative Therapies in Health and Medicine, 2015. **21**(5): p. 64–70.
19. McLean, H. S., Woodhose, A., Goldie, I., Cyhlarova, E. & Williamson, T., *An evidence review of the impact of participatory arts on older people.* 2011, Mental Health Foundation. https://www.mentalhealth.org.uk/publications/ evidence-review-impact-participatory-arts-older-people.
20. Perry, M., Maffully, N., Willson, S. & Morrissey, D., *The effectiveness of arts-based interventions in medical education: A literature review.* Medical Education, 2011. **45**(2): p. 141–148.

21. Acai, A., McQueen, S. A., McKinnon, V. & Sonnadara, R. R., *Using art for the development of teamwork and communication skills among health professionals: A literature review.* Arts & Health, 2017. **9**(1): p. 60–72.

22. Gordon-Nesbitt, R., *Exploring the longitudinal relationship between arts engagement and health.* 2015. Arts for Health, Manchester Metropolitan University. https://longitudinalhealthbenefits.wordpress.com/

23. Fancourt, D. & Steptoe, A., *Cultural engagement predicts changes in cognitive function in older adults over a 10 year period: Findings from the English Longitudinal Study of Ageing.* Scientific Reports, 2018. **8**(1): p. 10226.

24. Fancourt, D., Steptoe, A. & Cadar, D., *Cultural engagement and cognitive reserve: Museum attendance and dementia incidence over a 10-year period.* The British Journal of Psychiatry, 2018. **213**(5): p. 661–663.

25. Fancourt, D. & Tymoszuk, U., *Cultural engagement and incident depression in older adults: Evidence from the English Longitudinal Study of Ageing.* The British Journal of Psychiatry, 2018. **214**(4): p. 1–5.

26. Bygren, L. O., Konlaan, B. B. & Johansson, S. E., *Attendance at cultural events, reading books or periodicals, and making music or singing in a choir as determinants for survival: Swedish interview survey of living conditions.* BMJ, 1996. **313**: p. 1577–1580.

27. Węziak-Białowolska, D., *Attendance of cultural events and involvement with the arts impact evaluation on health and well-being from a Swiss household panel survey.* Public Health, 2016. **139**: p. 161–169.

28. Renton, A., Phillips, G., Daykin, N., Yu, G., Taylor, K. & Petticrew, M., *Think of your art-eries: Arts participation, behavioural cardiovascular risk factors and mental well-being in deprived communities in London.* Public Health, 2012. **126**(Suppl 1): p. S57–S64.

29. Guetzkow, J., *How the arts impact communities: An introduction to the literature on arts impact studies.* Centre for Arts and Cultural Policy Studies, Working Paper 20, 2002. Princeton University. https://www.princeton.edu/~artspol/workpap/WP20%20-%20Guetzkow.pdf

30. Matarasso, F., *Use or ornament? The social impact of participation in the arts.* 1997, Stroud: Comedia.

31. Putnam, R. D., *Bowling alone: The collapse and revival of American community.* 2000, New York: Simon & Schuster.

32. Putnam, R. D., *Democracies in flux: The evolution of social capital in contemporary society.* 2002, Oxford and New York: Oxford University Press.

33. Bourdieu, P., The forms of capital, in *The handbook of theory and research for the sociology of education*, J. G. Richardson (ed). 1986, New York: Greenwood. p. 241–258.

34. Osborne, K., Baum, F. & Zeirsch, A., *Negative consequences of community group participation for women's mental health and well-being: Implications for gender aware social capital building.* Journal of Community and Applied Social Psychology, 2009. **19**: p. 212–224.

35. Lee, L., *How the arts generate social capital to foster intergroup social cohesion.* The Journal of Arts Management, Law, and Society, 2013. **43**(1): p. 4–17.

36. Fujiwara, D., Kudrna, L. & Dolan, P., *Quantifying and valuing the wellbeing impacts of culture and sport.* 2014, London: Department of Culture, Media and Sport. https://www.gov.uk/government/publications/quantifying-and-valuing-the-wellbeing-impacts-of-culture-and-sport

37. Mansfield, L., Kay, T., Meads, C., John, A., Daykin, N., Grigsby Duffy, L., Lane, J., Dolan, P., Testoni, S., Julier, G., Payne, A., Tomlinson, A. & Victor, C., *A systematic review of outdoor recreation (in green space and blue space) for families to promote subjective wellbeing.* 2018, London: What Works Centre for Wellbeing. https://whatworkswellbeing.org/product/family-and-outdoor-recreation/

38. Pennington, A., Jones, R., Bagnall, A. M., South, J. & Corcoran, R., *Heritage and wellbeing: The impact of historic places and assets on community wellbeing-a scoping review.* 2019, London: What Works Centre for Wellbeing. https://whatworkswellbeing.org/product/heritage-and-wellbeing-full-scoping-review/

39. Victor, C., Mansfield, L., Kay, T., Daykin, N., Lane, J., Grigsby Duffy, L., Tomlinson, A. & Meads, C., *An overview of reviews: The effectiveness of interventions to address loneliness at all stages of the life-course.* 2018, London: What Works Centre for Wellbeing. https://whatworkswellbeing.org/product/tackling-loneliness-full-review/

4 Arts for health and community well-being: Examples from selected research studies

Introduction

This chapter discusses examples drawn from research studies on a range of arts projects and programmes in health and care. The case studies presented here are not intended as a representative sample; they are drawn from my own research and from studies I have undertaken with colleagues. However, they reflect a range of arts activities with different populations and in a range of settings, identifying issues and challenges that apply across many arts, health and well-being contexts. Each section begins with an overview of existing research on the topic before going on to discuss study findings and implications.

The role of visual arts and design in enhancing healthcare environments

The use of visual arts and music to enhance the healthcare environment is not new, but over the past 30 years, there has been increased awareness of the way in which the design of healthcare environments can improve the experiences of patients and staff as well as contributing to clinical outcomes and cost-effectiveness. Many hospitals have art collections and host exhibitions; they also engage artists and designers to help to improve wards and clinical areas as well as external gardens and landscaped areas [1]. There is a growing evidence base surrounding the use of arts and design in healthcare, which has been associated with a wide range of outcomes [2]. These include clinical effects including reduced stress, depression and anxiety, improved mood and distraction from worries, reduced falls in older people and improved wayfinding in dementia care. Staff report increased job satisfaction and enhanced perceptions of working conditions following arts and design interventions. Arts in healthcare environments are popular with patients and staff and may offer value for money, for instance, by contributing to reduced length of stay as well as a reduction in problems such as vandalism [3].

A key question is that of how hospital arts and design should be funded. In countries like the US, where healthcare is mostly funded through employer-based and publicly funded insurance schemes, investment in improved hospital design is often supported by business case arguments. The bulk of funding for US arts for health programmes has been provided by the operating budgets of organisations [4]. However, in systems that are funded largely from taxation, like the NHS, arts and design are sometimes viewed as non-essential luxuries or dismissed as a questionable priority. In many cases, hospital arts are funded by charitable donations, which means that resources are not equally distributed. This can lead to a concentration of arts in relatively affluent areas where more wealthy donors are concentrated.

Another issue relates to the aesthetic principles that should inform the design of healthcare environments. This is a challenging area to research, and the quality of the evidence is not consistent. It has been suggested that colours and images that are arousing may provoke anxiety, and that a preference for naturalistic environments over abstract art might fit with evolutionary psychological theories, although there is no universal agreement on this issue [5–8].

I explored these and other issues with colleagues in a qualitative study of the impact of a visual arts project in a mental health hospital environment [9]. The project involved 36 commissioned artworks such as integrated flooring, windows, water features, wall hangings, textiles and paintings, designed in consultation with service users, staff and other stakeholders across 16 new mental healthcare units as part of a modernisation project. The project sought to enhance the healthcare environment while enhancing service user participation. The research explored experiences of the project by patients, staff and artists using interviews, focus groups and documentary analysis. The study reported many benefits of arts and also revealed some underlying tensions that can affect mental healthcare environments, such as that between the two discourses of modernisation and participation. The former privileges 'prestige', and can be seen in the value placed on the engagement of highly regarded professional artists, while the latter favours notions of 'authenticity,' which places value on the extent to which artworks reflect or show empathy with the lived experience of mental health issues. In this project, service users were involved in the selection of artists, and the project included a participatory element. For a small number of staff and patients, this didn't go far enough towards true authenticity. This group sought protected opportunities for service users to claim and affirm non-stigmatised identities as 'artists' rather than 'patients'.

Despite these tensions, patients and staff spoke positively about their experience of the project and the final artworks. The research identified key processes through which arts could help to enhance patient and staff experiences of the environment, including modernisation, enhancing valued features, such as freedom and nature, diminishing negative aspects, such as routines and constraint, and providing creative opportunities through participation. We explored aesthetic preferences of participants, and there was general support for artworks and images that included reference to nature and locality, as well as the use of colour and light to create non-institutional imagery. However, beyond this, it wasn't possible to determine the inherent qualities of artworks that would render them popular or unpopular with patients and staff. Responses to the artworks were shaped by the interplay of aesthetic and contextual factors, including perceptions of the commissioning process. Nevertheless, we noted that service users tended to value arts outputs and processes where they felt an enhanced sense of control.

This research reinforced findings from previous research regarding the positive impact of visual arts and design on healthcare environments. It also revealed challenges, including funding and decisions about how resources should be allocated. The use of a qualitative methodology allowed us to explore process issues in depth, including tensions between competing discourses that could compound these challenges. It revealed the importance of issues of participation, authenticity and control in the design of mental healthcare environments. These issues of participation, authenticity and control also had a bearing on the research methodology. We found that service users who found it difficult to engage in focus groups and interviews often responded with enthusiasm when they were given an opportunity to show and discuss their own artworks. This highlights the importance of participatory arts, not just for improving healthcare environments but also for empowering and engaging participants in research and evaluation.

Music and arts in justice settings – the Musical Pathways Project

Provision of arts in criminal justice settings varies between countries and often fluctuates in response to changing policy and funding shifts as well as attitudes towards the balance between punishment and rehabilitation. However, the health, well-being and rehabilitation of offenders have been identified as a persistent public health issue. Justice settings face challenges arising from high levels of poor health and social exclusion of offenders, who tend to have poorer physical, mental and social health than the general population, with increased exposure to risks such as substance dependency, communicable diseases and violence [10]. A review of arts for young people in justice settings reported that young offenders present complex health and social needs including experiences of emotional trauma, lack of structured home environments and poor educational experiences [11].

There is a tradition of participatory arts for offenders in many countries, with activities such as painting, drawing, music making and creative writing provided by charities, small arts organisations, art therapists and volunteers [12,13]. Prison arts programmes can help to counter some of the health and well-being challenges that arise from incarceration, while evidence suggests that they benefit not only the incarcerated but also their families, the prison environment and society. Prison arts education can encourage attitudinal and behavioural changes, fostering increased self-confidence, motivation, self-discipline, emotional regulation, communication, creativity and intellectual flexibility [14]. For young offenders, music is seen as a particularly salient intervention that can promote healthy identity development and distract them from negative influences and crime. However, many challenges surround the delivery of arts and music activities in justice settings [15]. These are often fragmented, small-scale, short-term interventions that are difficult to evaluate. Projects such as music making for young offenders are often subject to moral panics surrounding genres that are seen to celebrate crime, for example, rap music and its association with sexism, misogyny and homophobia [11].

These issues were explored in our three-year study of music making for young offenders, led by Nick DeViggiani [16]. The music was led by a charity with long-standing experience of delivering projects in settings such as prisons, hospitals and healthcare settings. The programme involved over 100 young people aged 13–21 years in eight youth justice sites, including secure children's homes, juvenile secure units, young offender institutions and community-based youth offending teams. Music sessions of approximately two-hour duration were led for a period of six weeks by teams of two or three young professional musicians, most of whom who were trained in the conservatoire system and were highly skilled at performing, composing and producing music from a wide variety of genres. They introduced instruments such as guitars, keyboards, drums and percussion as well as woodwind and brass instruments and encouraged participants to sing, write songs and learn to play instruments. Participants worked towards informal performances for family members and prison staff as well as a final CD recording. They also had the opportunity to work with a professional artist to design CD covers.

In interviews and focus groups, participants reported many positive aspects of the programme, including its informality and fun, the distraction it provided from being in custody, the opportunity to feel safe, find expression and work productively in a group. We drew on deNora's concept of musical affordances to explore these impacts and the extent to which the young participants were able to access them within complex youth justice environments [17–20]. This suggests that music is not like a prescription drug, whose effects can be predicted in a dose-response relationship. Rather, musical affordances must be appropriated by participants in specific contexts.

The study revealed some of the challenges of delivering arts and music in these environments, which affected young peoples' engagement. These environments can seem chaotic and highly transient, with people constantly coming and going and participants often missing sessions due to institutional routines, resources and requirements. The success of the project was highly dependent on the supportive actions of staff in the different youth justice settings. They escorted musicians, participants and researchers within secure environments and remained present throughout sessions, often offering encouragement and praise to participants. The qualities, attitudes, skills and reflexive awareness of music leaders were also critically important. The social distance between them and project participants revealed itself in many ways: through different musical experiences, preferences, skills and attitudes. The young musicians needed to find points of connection at the same time as being able to navigate sensitivities surrounding language and behaviour as well as gender and sexual identities.

The study revealed the importance of goal setting in these environments. It also showed the high value that participants placed on artistic quality, as they perceived it. Production of the CD recording was a strong motivating factor for many young participants. However, different discourses of quality were reflected as the project progressed, beginning with brief displays of bravado and some inflexibility and intransigence shown by young people around the choice of music genre and performance style. The project was influenced by wider discourses of creativity, including ideas about innate talent and commercialism that can be problematic when it comes to well-being [21]. These were sometimes reflected in staff comments, such as when they sought to encourage participants using examples of famous people or popular TV talent shows. This contrasted with the more prosaic example set by the musicians, who modelled the benefits of dedicated personal study leading to portfolio working in the music industry. In the end, a situated definition of artistic quality emerged from these different elements, encouraged by musicians and many participants who ultimately valued genuine expression of life experiences more highly than stereotypical language and posturing. The most successful interactions were those that resulted in music that was meaningful to participants, transcending social differences and hegemonic ideas about creativity being the preserve of unique individuals and privileged elites. These processes were to a large extent shaped by fluctuating power relationships in often volatile, poorly resourced and oppressive environments.

This research reinforced existing findings about the benefits of arts and creativity within youth justice contexts. The use of ethnographic methods over three years enabled us to explore in depth the experiences of participants, identifying factors that frame engagement, leading to positive and negative impacts. The study revealed some of the issues that those leading projects need to consider, including how to manage the social distance between leaders and participants, how to negotiate relationships with powerful stakeholders in complex environments and how to find points of connection that do not reinforce stereotypes and divisions. The research illustrated the impact of wider discourses surrounding creativity and talent that can affect participants in arts and health projects. It not only highlights the importance of the quality of arts in these projects but also reveals the need for situated definitions of artistic quality informed by a critical understanding of specific contexts.

Community singing for health well-being

A text on arts, health and well-being would be incomplete without a discussion of community singing, the benefits of which are increasingly recognised in a burgeoning evidence base. The development of this subfield has been given impetus by a 15-year-long programme of international research undertaken by the Sidney De Haan Research Centre for Arts and Health at Canterbury Christ Church University [22]. Studies have examined the physiological effects of singing, for example, showing improved physical symptoms and quality of life in people with chronic obstructive pulmonary disease (COPD), although there is a need for larger studies with long-term follow-up [23–25].

Singing has also been identified with effects on mental well-being and quality of life across the life course [26–32]. A recent review used meta-analysis, a statistical technique to combine evidence from several studies that is rarely used in arts, health and well-being because of the heterogeneity of studies and outcomes, finding that singing is protective against the risk of depression in older people [26]. Singing is popular, and the growth of community singing for well-being has been encouraged by numerous recent TV programmes and media reports.

Experiences of community singing were explored in a questionnaire survey of participants in a choir programme provided for wives and partners of members of the British Armed Forces [33]. The choir sought to mitigate some of the demands and hardships associated with military life, including psychological stress and loneliness caused by long and unpredictable hours of duty, separation and periodic redeployments that disrupt friendships and links with community and the risk of injury or death. The study revealed perceptions of a wide range of benefits of participation. These include musical benefits, such as improved knowledge and skill, improvements in personal and social skills and experiences of bonding and social support. The project also reported personal, social, health and well-being benefits of participation, including strengthened social support, increased confidence and improved psychological well-being.

As well as these benefits, a small number of participants reported tensions and difficulties within choirs. Responses to open-ended questions revealed challenges of management and communication, the effects of internal politics and social hierarchies, pressures associated with performing and issues relating to repertoire. While some of the issues reported in this study are specific to military life, similar benefits and challenges have been documented in community music arts projects more generally.

Community arts and empowerment: a study of two genre-based music making projects

Community arts for health and well-being has been defined as a distinct area of activity operating outside of acute healthcare settings, often focused on the concerns of local people rather than the agendas of professionals and policy makers [34,35]. Community arts projects often seek to address issues of inequality and social inclusion and are distinguished by their commitment to social justice, a desire to seek transformational change rather than instrumental effects and a focus on relationship building through shared and ongoing reflective practice, issues and concerns, including inequalities and social exclusion. Although the funding climate for community arts is increasingly challenging in many countries, projects have proliferated since the first arts in community health projects appeared in the late 1980s, supported by a growing number of international networks and connections.

I worked with colleagues to explore these issues of community well-being in a study of two genre-based community music projects in contexts where there are higher than average health needs and well-being inequalities [36]. I had served as the Music Director of one of the projects and so the research included an element of reflective practice. Such projects may not be explicitly focused on health, rather, they follow the model of 'social action for music', exemplified, for example, in the Venezuelan El Sistema programme, established to offer opportunities and transformation through the provision of regular musical training in vulnerable and disadvantaged communities [37]. Relatively little research has been undertaken on this topic within the field of arts, health and well-being, although studies have addressed the broader impacts of community music [38].

The two projects included in the research were a community orchestra that focuses on reggae and a jazz big band, both operating in large cities with diverse, multi-ethnic populations. Both projects seek to celebrate the contributions of Black and minority ethnic (BME) musicians and composers identified as being otherwise marginalised in local music cultures and under-represented in the leadership of local cultural organisations. Both ensembles regularly engage between 35 and 40 male and female musicians from a wide range of backgrounds and rehearse regularly in local venues, with regular performances both locally and in their wider respective regions. They share similar operating procedures, for example, they maintain a flexible approach to the question of member subscriptions, raising money through a variety of means including charity fundraising. Neither group utilises auditions, and each offers regular coaching for members, as well as ongoing support of professional musicians and mentors.

The study sought to identify the benefits and challenges of participating in a community music ensemble and to explore project delivery and sustainability issues. An independent researcher undertook interviews with key participants and observed rehearsals and performances of both ensembles. These data were analysed, revealing common themes, despite the different needs that each ensemble seeks to address. Participants reported positive effects of participation on mood and mental well-being, with feelings of enjoyment, excitement and even euphoria after successful performances, as well as pride in their own achievements and in what the ensembles had brought to their respective communities. Participation enabled them to forge new musical connections and friendships, and music was described as breaking down barriers between people. There are also some negative aspects of participation, including technical and performance challenges, boredom, occasional disagreements about repertoire and performance values and feelings of sadness when established members moved on.

As Music Director I was aware of many challenges relating to community arts that seek to address inequalities by including marginalised populations. One of these relates to the complex meanings and significance that can be attached to specific genres, such as reggae. Many communities have a strong connection to cultural heritage, and music is often a valued community asset. People may feel protective towards 'their' music and may seek to resist its perceived appropriation by outside forces. For example, within the reggae project, some participants expressed a strong sense of 'ownership' of the reggae genre and voiced a desire for the music to be performed in traditional ways. However, other members wanted to explore the boundaries of the genre, creating new forms that reflected current local living conditions including more recent phases of migration from Europe and work with refugees from countries such as Somalia, Iran and the Sudan. Discussions within the group often focused on the extent to which the project should be a heritage project and the scope and limits of innovation. Eventually, the project successfully combined development of new fusions such as 'Persian reggae' and 'Sudanese reggae' with performance of traditional Jamaican reggae standards.

These debates reflect tensions discussed previously between bonding and bridging capital [39,40]. They illustrate the way in which the former can support well-being by reinforcing a shared sense of identity and an awareness of cultural assets. However, bonding doesn't necessarily promote broader connections unless a conscious effort is made through bridging. Hence, leaders of community music projects that seek to engage with disadvantaged communities need to be aware of both bridging and bonding capital, respecting musical traditions and building trust while being open to musical explorations and new connections that can widen opportunities for members and communities. With this in mind, the research suggests that membership of community ensemble can afford many creative and educational opportunities as well as supporting the well-being of members and contributing to a wider sense of empowerment in the communities from which they are drawn.

Conclusions

The studies discussed here illustrate some of the issues that arise in different contexts were arts activities are used to enhance health and well-being. As well as positive impacts, project challenges have also been explored within these studies. The findings suggest that the domain of arts, health and well-being is framed by shifting discourses and shaped by macro-, meso- and micro-level forces. At the macro level are questions of funding and resources that structure the context in which participatory arts for health and well-being takes place. While the field of arts, health and well-being is growing, it faces substantial funding challenges, and broader questions remain about how to resource it in the longer term. Many of the activities discussed here were funded from charitable sources. This can lead to instability and a preponderance of short-term projects, making it difficult to challenge inequalities in a sustained way. Another issue is the way in which funding support for projects fluctuates with changing political attitudes. This affects many fields, although it is most strongly apparent in criminal justice settings, where projects are affected by changing attitudes about punishment and rehabilitation or by moral panics surrounding genres that are viewed as contributing to anti-social behaviour.

The meso level refers to the institutional and organisational frameworks that shape project delivery. The research studies here reveal the way in which the success of arts activities and programmes is often contingent on institutional roles, routines and imperatives. The responses of gatekeepers, including professionals, who themselves are often navigating strongly hierarchical environments, are a critical factor. While individual staff are often positive about the arts, in their role as gatekeepers and observers, they can limit projects in conscious and unconscious ways, for example, by introducing notions of art and creativity, such as received ideas from popular culture, that may conflict with the goals of arts for health and well-being.

Project experiences can be shaped by social divisions and inequalities that affect micro-level relationships. For some participants, engagement in arts is limited by health and mobility impairments and by other challenges, such as working patterns, availability of transport and access to other resources. It can also be constrained by differences in social and educational backgrounds, revealed in different expectations, preferences and beliefs about arts. The failure to successfully navigate these differences can serve to reinforce stereotypes and divisions, including those based on class, gender, ethnicity and sexual identity. In fact, many arts and health practitioners demonstrate high levels of sensitivity and skill in this area, but these skills tend to be developed through experience and are addressed to varying degrees in the initial arts education. A common finding in these research studies is that the success of arts projects is highly contingent on the qualities, attitudes, skills and reflexive awareness of leaders.

The discussion also sheds light on the importance of aesthetic values and artistic quality. One question that many participatory projects encounter is that of who is entitled to be designated an 'artist' and who decides? In some projects, the production of an output that participants perceived as high quality, such as a music recording, is a strong motivating factor for participants. Yet several studies point to the fact that quality is socially constructed and emergent from specific project experiences rather than being guided by universal principles imposed from the outside.

Finally, this chapter has discussed the capacity of arts projects to address health and well-being inequalities, focusing on tensions between bonding and bridging social capital. Music and arts represent valuable community assets, particularly for members of disadvantaged communities who may have a strong investment in a shared cultural heritage. Project design should reflect this, and arts practitioners need to demonstrate sensitivity, avoiding cultural misappropriation whilst fostering openness and innovation in order to forge broader connections and increase the opportunities and resources available to participants.

The research discussed in this chapter has explored impacts of arts as well as the factors that shape project outcomes and processes. Another set of questions surrounds the broader development of the field, including questions of scope, such as how to scale up interventions to benefit wider groups of people, and how to develop the field to reflect artistic perspectives and value participant experiences. Alternative frameworks to those drawn from quantitative and qualitative healthcare evaluation are needed to address these challenges. The following two chapters explore theories and frameworks from social science and organisational studies, including social movement theory, which is increasingly viewed by policy leaders as the key to addressing critical challenges in health and care.

References

1. Lambert, P. D., ed., *Managing arts programs in healthcare*. 2016, London: Routledge.
2. Daykin, N., Byrne, E., Soteriou, T. & O'Connor, S., *The impact of art, design and environment in mental healthcare: A systematic review of the literature*. Journal of the Royal Society for the Promotion of Health, 2008. **128**(2): p. 85–94.

3. Francis, S., Willis, J. & Garvey, A., *Improving the patient experience evaluation of the King's Fund's Enhancing the Healing Environment programme.* 2003, London: The Kings Fund, NHS Estates and The Stationary Office.

4. Sonke, J., Rollins, J., Brandman, R. & Graham-Pole, J., *The state of arts in healthcare in the United States.* Arts and Health: An International Journal of Research, Policy and Practice, 2009. **1**(2): p. 107–135.

5. Cusack, P., Fremantle, C., Isles, C. & Lankston, L., *Visual art in hospitals: Case studies and review of the evidence.* Journal of the Royal Society of Medicine, 2010. **103**(12): p. 490–499.

6. Ulrich, R. S. & Gilpin. L., Healing arts: Nutrition for the soul, in *Putting patients first: Designing and practicing patient-centred care*, L. Gilpin, S. B. Frampton & P. A. Charmel (eds). 2003, San Francisco, CA: Jossey-Bass. p. 117–146.

7. Ulrich, R., Quan, X., Zimring, C., Joseph, A. & Choudhary, R., *The role of the physical environment in the hospital of the 21st century: A once-in-a-lifetime opportunity. Report to the Center for Health Design for the Designing the 21st Century Hospital Programme.* 2004, Concord, CA: Center for Health Design.

8. Nielsen, S.L., Fich, L.B., Roessler, K. K. & Mullins, M. F. *How do patients actually experience and use art in hospitals? The significance of interaction: A user-oriented experimental case study.* International Journal of Qualitative Studies in Health and Well-being, 2017. **12**(1): p. 1267343. doi:10.1080/17482631.2016.1267343.

9. Daykin, N., Byrne, E., Soteriou, T. & O'Connor, S., *Using arts to enhance mental healthcare environments: Findings from qualitative research, arts & health.* Arts and Health: An International Journal for Research, Policy and Practice, 2010. **2**(1): p. 33–46.

10. Hayton, P., Protecting and promoting health in prisons: A settings approach, in *Health in prisons. A WHO guide to the essentials in prison health.* H. S. Lars Møller, R. Jürgens, A. Gatherer & H. Nikogosian (eds). 2007, Copenhagen: WHO Regional Office for Europe.

11. Daykin, N., de Viggiani, N., Pilkington, P. & Moriarty, Y., *Music making for health, well-being and behaviour change in youth justice settings: A systematic review.* Health Promotion International, 2013. **28**(2): p. 197–210.

12. de Quadros, A., Case study: 'I once was lost but now am found' – Music and embodied arts in two American prisons, in *Oxford textbook of creative arts, health, and wellbeing*, S. Clift & P. M. Camic (eds). 2016, Oxford: Oxford University Press. p. 187–192.

13. Robertson, T., Case study: Creativity in criminal justice settings – The work of the Koestler Trust, in *Oxford textbook of creative arts, health, and wellbeing*, S. Clift & P. M. Camic (eds). 2016, Oxford: Oxford University Press. p. 291–297.

14. Brewster, L., *The impact of prison arts programs on inmate attitudes and behavior: A quantitative evaluation.* Justice Policy Journal, 2014. **11**(2). p. 1–28.

15. Kubrin, C. E., *'I see death around the corner' Nihilism in rap music.* Sociological Perspectives, 2006. **48**: p. 433–459.

16. Daykin, N., de Viggiani, N., Moriarty, Y. & Pilkington, P., *Music-making for health and wellbeing in youth justice settings: Mediated affordances and the impact of context and social relations.* Sociology of Health and Illness, 2017. **39**(6): p. 941–958.

17. DeNora, T., *Music in everyday life.* 2000, Cambridge: Cambridge University Press.

18. DeNora, T., *After adorno: Rethinking music sociology.* 2003, Cambridge: Cambridge University Press.

19. DeNora, T., *Music asylums. Wellbeing through music in everyday life.* 2015, Farnham: Ashgate.

20. Ansdell, G., *How music helps in music therapy and everyday life.* 2016, London and New York: Routledge.

21. Daykin, N., *Disruption, dissonance and embodiment: Creativity, health and risk in music narratives.* Health (London), 2005. **9**(1): p. 67–87.

22. Clift, S., Hancox, G., Morrison, I., Skingley, A. & Vella-Burrows, T., Group singing as a public health resource, in *Oxford textbook of creative arts, health and wellbeing*, S. Clift & P. M. Camic (eds). 2016. Oxford: Oxford University Press. p. 3–10.

23. McNamara, R. J, Epsley, R. J., Coren, E. & McKeought, Z.J., *Singing for adults with chronic obstructive pulmonary disease.* Cochrane Database of Systematic Reviews. 2017. doi:10.1002/14651858.CD012296.pub2

24. Lewis, A., Cave, P., Stern, M., Welch, L., Taylor, K., Russell, J., Doyle, A. M., Russell, A. M., McKee, H., Clift, S., Bott, J. & Hopkinson, N. S., *Singing for lung health: A systematic review of the literature and consensus statement.* NPJ Primary Care Respiratory Medicine, 2016. **26**: p. 16080.

25. Skingley, A., Clift, S., Hurley, S., Price, S. & Stephens, L., *Community singing groups for people with chronic obstructive pulmonary disease: Participant perspectives.* Perspectives in Public Health. **138**(1): p. 66–75.

26. Daykin, N., Mansfield, L., Meads, C., Julier, G., Tomlinson, A., Payne, A., Grigsby Duffy, L., Lane, J., D'Innocenzo, G., Burnett, A., Kay, T., Dolan, P., Testoni, S. & Victor, C., *What works for wellbeing? A systematic review of wellbeing outcomes for music and singing in adults.* Perspect Public Health, 2018. **138**(1): p. 39–46.

27. Fancourt, D. & Perkins, R., *Associations between singing to babies and symptoms of postnatal depression, wellbeing, self-esteem and mother-infant bond.* Public Health, 2017. **145**: p. 149–152.

28. Fancourt, D. & Perkins, R., *Effect of singing interventions on symptoms of postnatal depression: Three-arm randomised controlled trial.* The British Journal of Psychiatry, 2018. **212**(2): p. 119–121.

29. Warran, K., Fancourt, D. & Wiseman, T., *How does the process of group singing impact on people affected by cancer? A grounded theory study.* BMJ Open, 2019. **9**(1): p. e023261.

30. Perkins, R., Yorke, S. & Fancourt, D., *How group singing facilitates recovery from the symptoms of postnatal depression: A comparative qualitative study.* BMC Psychology, 2018. **6**(1): p. 41.

31. Victor, C., Daykin, N., Mansfield, L., Payne, A., Grigsby Duffy, L., Lane, J., Julier, G., Tomlinson, A. & Meads, C., *Music, singing and wellbeing for adults living with dementia.* 2016, London: What works wellbeing.
32. Skingley, A. & Vella-Burrows, T., *Therapeutic effects of music and singing for older people.* Nursing Standard, 2010. **24**(19): p. 35–41.
33. Clift, S., Page, S., Daykin, N. & Peasgood, E., *The perceived effects of singing on the health and well-being of wives and partners of members of the British Armed Forces: A cross-sectional survey.* Public Health, 2016. **138**: p. 93–100.
34. White, M., The means to flourish: Arts in community health and education, in *Oxford textbook of creative arts, health, and wellbeing*, S. Clift & P. M. Camic (eds). 2016, Oxford: Oxford University Press. p. 41–48.
35. White, M., *A social tonic: The development of arts in community health.* 2009, Oxford: Radcliffe.
36. Tapson, C., Daykin, N. & Walters, D., *The role of genre-based community music: A study of two UK ensembles.* International Journal of Community Music, 2018. **11**(3): p. 289–309.
37. Creech, A., Gonzalez-Moreno, P., Lorenzino, L. & Waitman, G., Case study: Lost – or found?- in translation. The globalization of Venezuela's El Sistema, in *Oxford textbook of creative arts, health, and wellbeing*, S. Clift & P. M. Camic (eds). 2016, Oxford: Oxford University Press. p. 193–198.
38. Higgins, L., *Community music: In theory and in practice.* 2012, New York: Oxford University Press and Oxford University Press.
39. Putnam, R. D., *Bowling alone: The collapse and revival of American community.* 2000, New York: Simon & Schuster. p. 541.
40. Putnam, R. D., *Democracies in flux: The evolution of social capital in contemporary society.* 2002, Oxford and New York: Oxford University Press. p. 516.

5 Arts, health and well-being as a social movement

Introduction

The previous chapter suggested that the development of the field of arts, health and well-being raises underlying questions that cannot be answered by evidence alone. For example, how much evidence is needed to justify investment in an arts project or programme in health and care? What kind of evidence should be prioritised in policy making? Which underlying frameworks should guide evaluation? To what extent should arts and health research adhere to hierarchies of evidence used in healthcare? How should the experiences of project participants be reflected in research? How can the voices of and stand-points of artists help to shape research agendas? Ultimately, these are political and moral questions that are unlikely to be resolved by improvements in methodologies alone. They demand attention to the sociopolitical context in which decisions about arts, health and care are made. One potentially useful framework, which has attracted the recent attention of healthcare leaders, is that of social movement the-ory, developed within social science and organisational studies.

The broad network of interactions and energies surrounding arts, health and well-being has often been described as a social move-ment, for example, by Clive Parkinson in his blog post on the devel-opment of the movement in the North West of England [1]. Likewise, the 2013 Royal Society of Public Health (RSPH) report, 'Arts, Health and Wellbeing Beyond the Millennium: How far have we come and where do we want to go?' documents the growth of the 'arts and health movement' (p. 7) [2]. This is linked with a broader programme of ho-listic healthcare models emphasising health promotion, prevention, well-being and reducing inequalities, beginning with the 1986 Ottawa Charter (https://www.who.int/healthpromotion/conferences/previous/ottawa/en/), which presented the World Health Organization's (WHO)

Health for All strategy. Social movement theory may provide a useful tool with which to examine the broader context of arts, health and well-being research, policy and practice.

Social movement theory

Social movements have been defined as networks of informal interactions between individuals and groups engaged in political or cultural conflicts based on their shared collective identities and purpose [3]. Social movements are usually led from below to challenge powerful groups and vested interests, such as the recent example 'Occupy Wall Street' protests that combined anti-consumerist elements with ideas about social justice and democracy [4]. However, they can also be reformist or conservative or led by elites and vested interests seeking to resist demands such as regulation on issues such as the environment, health and public protection [3].

According to Tilly, social movements are not necessarily coherent groups with clear aims, but they are clearly distinguishable from other groupings and forms of social action, such as interest groups and political campaigns, by the presence of three populations: power holders who are the object of claims, participants, who range from minor contributors to leaders, and a subject population on whose behalf participants are making or supporting claims [5]. While social class is strongly implicated in many health issues that are the subject of social movement activism, social movements can include a wide range of cultural groups and identities [6]. Whatever their degree of radicalism, a sense of grievance has been identified as a defining characteristic for a social movement [7].

A social movement consists of:

> a sustained challenge to power holders in the name of a population living under the jurisdiction of those power holders by means of repeated public displays of that population's worthiness, unity, numbers, and commitment. At a minimum, social movements involve continuous interaction between challengers and power holders. [5] (p. 257)

Health social movements (HSMs) are part of a long tradition that began with attempts to improve living and working conditions following the industrial revolution [6–8]. Early social movements focused on issues such as occupational health and regulation of the workplace. Among public health researchers, there is a consensus that many historical advances, such as the reduced impact of infectious diseases on life expectancy and health in developed societies, are attributable to improved social conditions such as diet and hygiene, rather than to scientific and medical discoveries [9,10]. Hence, social movements have played an important role in health improvement, and they continue to do so by challenging interests such as the transglobal tobacco, alcohol or food manufacturing industries. HSMs often converge around and reframe embodied experiences, campaigning against stigma and discrimination in areas such as mental health, HIV/AIDs, women's health, dementia and disability. Social movements seek to make changes in society, not just individual experience, and they often challenge decision-making in policy, as well as in research funding and the practices of evidence production [11].

Health as a social movement

Recent thinking about social movements has shifted away from a focus on contentious politics and grievances to emphasise the potential for the energies of social movements to be harnessed to address problems and challenges in health and care. Hence, while social movements have been traditionally associated with the mobilisation of people to achieve radical social change, Burbidge suggests a more nuanced view based on the concept of energy arising from the interactions between individuals, communities and organisations that can be constructively used and spread for the purposes of change. This energy need not be negative or combative, rather this can be harnessed to fuel grass-roots, community-led action that addresses local needs such as transport, services and facilities for older people living alone [12].

Similarly, a recent report by NESTA suggests that social movements are an integral part of a healthy and thriving society, linking low social movement activity with institutional dominance and fatalism, and high social movement activity with active citizenship and diversity [13]. However, the authors suggest that high social movement activity can also indicate a plethora of grievances, and if met with low institutional agility, it can lead to an environment of societal discontent, agitation and protest. Hence, health services that meet high social movement activity with institutional agility are needed to create new levels of innovation, transformation and growth co-led by people and institutions (p. 19).

This way of thinking links social movement theory with current policy emphasis on asset-based approaches to health and care, with a growing view that 'community assets and social action are part of the solution to preventing ill health' [14] (p. 6). Policy makers have increasingly turned their attention to social movements, adopting an asset-based approach in which movements and actors can help to mitigate rising pressures on services. Responding to current demographic and health challenges such as increased prevalence of chronic physical and mental ill health and widening health inequalities requires new people-centred ways of thinking that can foster relational rather than hierarchical forms of power and leadership and engage people at grass-roots level to solve problems. An example of this kind of thinking can be seen in NHS England's 2014 Five Year Forward View, which declares an ambition to build a social movement to empower communities to address the health issues they face at the same time as mitigating demands on services [15]. A social movement approach has been adopted, initially in six vanguard sites, fostering different kinds of local action including volunteering, advocacy, co-production, community asset ownership and community organising. One of the projects is Stockport Together, which seeks to tackle loneliness and social isolation in the Greater Manchester area of the UK. As part of the programme, people are encouraged to take part in creative activities such as storytelling and film making within their communities, supported by an existing Live Well Make Art network.

The adoption of social movement approaches by policy leaders raises key questions about power and belonging in social movements. While many social movements have been borne out of shared experiences, not all members of social movements have direct experience of a specified health condition or social challenge, and many HSMs include supporters and allies. In more broadly focused movements, the actions of government officials, researchers, scientists and other stakeholders also contribute to a shared cultural programme, and social movements often seek to benefit from external opportunities and resources by forging alliances with sympathetic leaders [3,7,16,17]. More recent work emphasises the two-way nature of these relationships, advocating collaboration and joint working to solve shared problems, although these authors warn against the simple exploitation of community assets to fulfil policy agendas [12,13].

The evaluators of NHS England's vanguard programme acknowledge that the idea of policy makers leading social movements is counter-intuitive [14] (p. 34). Critical challenges arise from attempts to forge artificial connections that serve policy agendas and draw on the energies of local people, who are often those in society with the least capacity to solve problems, without addressing existing hierarchical power structures. As Burbidge suggests, such interactions can quickly become negative and drain energy. Without fair and transparent processes, it can feel that the power of the state is being used unfairly in impenetrable processes. Successful social movements can potentially change the culture that shapes local services, but this requires policy makers give space for social movements to flourish and invest in the development of genuine connections as well as a shared vision, language and culture. This requires new forms of leadership based on entrepreneurial action that is flexible, responsive and strongly engaged with people, communities and professionals working within existing services and institutions. Such entrepreneurs can inspire and forge meaningful connections between change agents including innovators, champions, opinion leaders, boundary spanners and ordinary people [12] (p. 10). The qualities of effective social movement leaders have also been discussed by del Castillo et al., who suggest that there are five primary capacities: forging new relationships, framing issues to ensure broad commitment, devising strategies, catalysing action and developing capacity in others [13].

A brief history of the arts and health 'movement'

In the context of this debate, the field of arts, health and well-being exhibits many characteristics of a social movement. Its members include grass-roots organisations and individuals, but policy leaders have also played a key role in its development. For example, in the UK, the RSPH, an independent health charity that seeks to improve and protect public health and well-being, has for several years brought together artists, project participants, researchers, health professionals and researchers, most recently through its Arts, Health and Wellbeing Special Interest Group (SIG). This group has an international membership and is supported by a steering group drawn from research, policy and practice. It seeks to promote evidence-based approaches to arts in healthcare by sharing information, organising events and influencing policy as a professional body.

Social movement thinking has influenced the development of the arts and health field. Hence, the narrative of the 2013 RSPH report presents the growth of a progressive movement over the last 30 years [2]. It discusses key events such as the Windsor Conferences in 1998 and 1999, which advocated for a culture shift in the delivery of healthcare and articulated an agenda for the movement. The Windsor Declaration included a 12-point Action Plan covering professional education, arts therapy in healthcare settings and arts in community development, health and well-being. If arts and health is a social movement, its aims are to elevate the arts in each of these fields in order to contribute to specific clinical goals, educate professionals to become more compassionate and intuitive, empower patients and communities and combat social exclusion [18].

The sense of arts and health as a movement has been reinforced through campaigning, advocacy and networking events. For example, international conferences on Culture, Health and Wellbeing were held in Bristol, first UK in June 2013 and again in 2017. The 2013 conference was the first of its kind, bringing together 390 delegates and speakers from 22 countries including Australia, New Zealand, Japan, Canada, USA, Nigeria, South Africa, Finland and Sweden, to explore the role of arts in relation to key themes of promoting healthy and creative ageing, reducing global health inequalities and addressing the social determinants of well-being. Delegates were drawn from a wide range of arts sectors including museums, galleries, performing arts, visual arts, arts therapies and community arts. They spanned a range of disciplines including mental health, public health, psychology, sociology, arts, humanities and medicine. They included artists, researchers, cultural directors, charity workers, community participants, grass-roots activists and healthcare professionals. As well as keynote presentations from senior policy makers and public health specialists, there were performances by international artists such as Japanese vocalist Sizzle Ohtaka, and a performance by the Irish Chamber Orchestra of Ian Wilson's 'Bewitched', composed during a residency in the stroke unit at Tallaght Hospital, Dublin. The conference sought to showcase cutting edge research, but unlike traditional academic conferences, peer review research papers were presented alongside practice case studies and experiential workshops, creating a strong sense of cross-disciplinary engagement to connect academic, experiential and lay knowledge. The notion of arts and health as a social movement was reinforced by the keynote presentation by Lord Howarth of Newport who gave an impassioned call to action, encouraging conference delegates to create a manifesto, to advocate for the effectiveness and cost-effectiveness of the arts and to persuade policy makers, practitioners and commissioners of key facts, such as that the arts are loved by patients and frail elderly people as well as by health and care staff. Although it would be a 'long march', this approach would eventually succeed in, 'changing practice, improving the culture, developing a new wisdom' in which arts are an accepted part of health and care delivery [19] (p. 7).

The contribution of policy leaders was apparent following the conference, at which the UK All Party Parliamentary Group for Arts, Health and Wellbeing (APPGAHW) was launched. This group connected experts and lay people with parliamentarians and organised a two-year inquiry, resulting in the report, 'Creative Health' [20]. The report made several recommendations, including the establishment of a central coordinating organisation to promote the development of the field. Subsequently, the Culture, Health and Wellbeing Alliance (CHWA) was launched. Similar developments have taken place in countries such as Finland, through the establishment of Taikysydän, a coordination and leadership organisations such as which collects and disseminate knowledge about good practice and evidence in arts, health and well-being.

As a social movement, arts, health and well-being appears to have been successful in making arts-based approaches more visible and credible to policy makers. Recently, the expansion of policy developments such as social prescribing has brought many arts projects and programmes into focus. Leaders have supported the development of frameworks for arts commissioning through initiatives like Public Health England's Arts and Health Evaluation Framework [21]. Arts organisations have increasingly embraced the theme of health and well-being, while many non-governmental organisations (NGOs), third sector and commercial organisations have increased their activity in this area. Research funding organisations have begun to recognise the place of the arts and humanities in addressing social and health problems within interdisciplinary calls for funding. An early career research network established in 2013 now has over one thousand members from 30 countries (https://www.artshealthecrn.com/).

Despite these successes, arts are still a long way from being embedded within healthcare systems, and the sector faces ongoing challenges. It remains relatively fragmented, made up of small organisations and individuals competing for ever-diminishing funds. While there have been regular calls for 'scaling up' and standardisation of arts for health programmes, there is no universal agreement about whether and how this should be done. Further, many artists and project participants struggle to engage with healthcare systems, often feeling overwhelmed and disempowered by scientific and medical culture and language [22]. This links with uncertainties about how best to evaluate practice and how to utilise evidence and research frameworks. These challenges reflect underlying tensions between top-down and bottom-up approaches to social movement growth.

Is arts and health a social movement?

The field of arts, health and well-being is diverse, drawing together artists, participants, grass-roots activists, professionals, managers, researchers, entrepreneurs and policy makers. Some, such as the leaders of large healthcare or cultural organisations, seem relatively powerful, but the field is also driven by the actions of small, independent organisations and individuals. The field encompasses a relatively devalued arts and cultural sector as well as the voices of vulnerable people in relatively low prestige areas of medicine, such as mental health. The motivations of stakeholders in arts, health and well-being reflect their diverse interests and histories. Some are motivated by personal experience, while others are driven by professional concerns. Some seek to resolve specific clinical problems, while others are drawn more broadly to arts-based approaches as a form of innovation in response to mounting pressures on health and care services. A small number operate from commercial interests, while a growing number are influenced by political, organisational and strategic goals. Many emphasise a rights-based approach to arts, culture and well-being, advocating socially engaged arts practice as a way of challenging elitist notions of 'high art' in favour of community involvement and social inclusion [23].

According to Tilly, it is a mistake to see every initiative with movement-like qualities as a social movement [5]. Here we have discussed the defining characteristics of social movements, which are essentially networks of informal interactions between individuals and groups engaged in sustained challenges to power holders based on their shared collective identities and purpose. Social movements may differ in their degree of radicalism and sense of grievance, but a key characteristic is that they offer collective challenges to policy and practice. The notion of arts and health as a social movement is supported by its history of over 20 years of sustained interaction, network and advocacy addressed at identified sources of power, including health policy makers and arts and cultural sector leaders. Over this period, a sense of collective identity has been forged through conferences, networking events and meetings. Stakeholders have knowledge and research, developed resources such as journals, databases and websites, lobbied and engaged consistently with the leaders of policy, service and research organisations. They are drawn together by a shared conviction that health and care services should incorporate the power of creativity to address a wide range of needs. Beyond that, there is no single agenda or coherent purpose. However, this is true of many social movements.

Importantly, the arts, health and well-being movement draws its energies from the actions of grass-roots projects and participants. However, key organisations and leaders have provided support and advocacy, often with a view to convincing policy makers of the value of creativity. This broadly fits with Burbidge's energy-focused perspective in which the interactions between individuals, communities and organisations engaged in social movements offer a conduit for innovation and change [12], but it perhaps falls short of a coherent challenge to policy and practice frameworks. Some would argue that arts and health as a movement should present a more radical agenda driven by a bottom-up approach focused on empowerment and explicitly engaged with political economy issues.

These issues are discussed in a blog post by Clive Parkinson, who describes the effects of the global financial crisis on the emergent arts and health movement in the North West of England [1]. The crash in 2008 disrupted a steady process of growing relationships and connections between artists, public health professionals, academics, activists and community participants. These had developed steadily from a rich vein of grass-roots arts activity, but following the crash, arts projects and programmes have been negatively and disproportionately affected by financial crises and funding constraints. Frustrated with the direction of economic policies and their effects on the poor, Parkinson produced a manifesto for arts and health based on a shared vision and aspirations of this emergent community [24]. The manifesto positions the arts at the centre of a broader movement for radical social change, opposing austerity-driven public policies and rejecting individualist and consumerist notions of arts. The manifesto resists the idea of arts as a panacea for social problems or an adjunct to clinical care. Rather, it suggests that arts for health as a social movement has the potential to challenge mainstream economic and social policies by strengthening the voices of disempowered people and placing culture at the heart of decision-making.

Whether or not arts, health and well-being is considered a social movement, social movement theory offers useful insights into key challenges facing the field. These include strategies for development, issues of propagation and scale and questions surrounding research, advocacy and evaluation. These are discussed in the following section.

Development, propagation and scale in arts, health and well-being

The field of arts, health and well-being is relatively fragmented, with not only pockets of excellent practice but also gaps and barriers to developing sustainable projects that can tackle health and well-being inequalities. Fragmentation, piecemeal development and the increasing reliance on charitable funding makes it difficult to ensure that high-quality arts reach the geographical areas and population groups that would benefit the most from them. A number of scenarios have been advocated to allow programmes to expand and achieve sustainability, including supporting organisational development, creating coordinating and leadership bodies, securing the engagement of key policy and arts sector leaders, providing training and professional regulation for artists, standardising evaluation frameworks and scaling up of projects and programmes using traditional business models such as franchising. However, no consensus has been reached about whether these strategies to achieve standardisation and scale should be adopted [22].

Studies of the trajectories and impacts of social movements may help to understand these issues. According to Tilly, social movements do not have continuous, self-contained life histories, and it is unlikely that general laws of how they work can be identified. Nevertheless, they do lay down coherent histories within their boundaries [4]. Discussions about what determines the effectiveness of a social movement's work have focused on organisational development, charting phases of emergence, coalescence, bureaucratisation and decline [25]. They have also identified reasons for the failure of social movements, such as problems arising from internal divisions and factionalism [26]. However, the decline of a social movement can be result of success as well as failure, as this may indicate that its aims have been achieved or its goals and ideas adopted by the mainstream [17]. For example, an arts and health 'movement' may become redundant or shift its purpose if the aim of fully integrating arts-based approaches within health and care was achieved.

Social movement theory has also examined the way in which movements propagate and grow. According to Burbidge, they do this across the two dimensions: actions and ideologies [12]. Regarding actions, propagation occurs as the strategies and tactics of social movements are spread and replicated in other sites. Regarding ideologies, movements spread their ideas and framing of issues, goals and aspirations. Hence, even if social movements fall short of their stated objectives, they can inspire people and help to change policy discourse if their concerns and actions resonate with people in different contexts [4]. Examples of propagation in arts, health and well-being include cultural commissioning and social prescribing, where successful delivery models have been piloted, disseminated and adopted in different geographical areas and settings. Another example is that of singing for well-being, with the proliferation of well-being choirs following popular TV programmes and media reports of the benefits of singing. However, propagation and scale can be highly dependent on relationships, including interpersonal connections and informal networks. Hence, arts-based approaches to health and well-being do not lend themselves to simple reproduction: they often respond to specific needs and local circumstances.

Social movement theory and research challenges in arts, health and well-being

Social movement theory also offers some useful insights into research challenges facing the field. One characteristic that the arts, health and well-being field shares with documented social movements is its paradoxical relationship with research and evidence [3,8]. Social movements often challenge mainstream scientific and research priorities, including hierarchies of evidence. On the other hand, they also seek to harness scientific knowledge and resources, utilising and building on traditional forms of evidence in order to advocate for changes in policy and resource allocation.

These tensions are apparent in research on arts, health and well-being. A Delphi study, undertaken as part of the underpinning research for the What Works Centre for Wellbeing Culture and Sport Evidence Review Programme, examined a wide range of stakeholder perspectives on best practice in research and quality of evidence [27]. The study found that beyond a broad agreement that evidence is needed to support funding of cultural and sports projects and programmes in health and care, there is a lack of consensus about how to evaluate these, with disagreement about the extent to which hierarchies of evidence and frameworks drawn from medicine and health should be applied. Some stakeholders from the arts and cultural sectors argued that evidence based healthcare frameworks disempower artists, devalue the processes at work in arts activities and diminish participants' stories and experiences.

Balancing these potentially conflicting perspectives involves strategies that can create additional problems. For example, one strategy adopted by social movements is to gain a closer relationship with knowledge production by engaging with scientific models and organisations. However, this can involve difficult trade-offs, as Epstein's account of the role of AIDS activism in reforming clinical trial protocols during the 1980s and 1990s demonstrates. This study explored the way in which movement activists sought to gain a foothold and play a part in the construction of scientific knowledge by acquiring cultural competence and adopting technical language in order to engage with scientific communities. They also achieved success in influencing scientific research agendas by exploiting and taking sides with pre-existing arguments within scientific communities. Hence, they aligned themselves with debates about how clinical trials should be organised, supporting those scientists who were in favour of 'pragmatic' as opposed to 'fastidious' research designs [28,29]. This kind of strategy risks replicating the expert/lay division within the ranks of social movement activists, leaving them open to accusations of co-option and conservatism. According to Epstein, problems arose from two broad movement goals that were ambiguously defined. The first goal of trying to improve research and evidence by eliminating biases that led to marginalisation of particular health issues and constituencies was in conflict with the second, of challenging epistemological foundations of scientific practice [11].

Similar tensions are reflected within the arts and health 'movement' in discussions about research and evaluation strategies. In response to statements that the evidence base for arts, health and well-being is relatively weak, a growing number of projects and publications adopt what are viewed as increasingly robust methodologies. Tools and resources have been developed to support improved evaluation research, such as a version of the Medical Research Council's framework for evaluating complex intervention, adapted for the arts and health sector [30]. While such resources can be helpful, we have noted claims that arts-based epistemologies are overlooked and that such frameworks and tools can be insensitive to the nuances of artistic experience. The trade-off here is that while aligning closely with medically based evidence hierarchies may gain the attention of policy makers, it may also distort research and overlook the concerns of participants, artists and grass-roots activists whose outcomes may not readily map onto the health improvements that policy makers and researchers seek to measure [31] (p. 111). The late Mike White warned against stifling the emergent vision and potential of arts and health by only seeking a proven evidence base that is narrowly defined through controlled studies [23].

Social movement theory reminds us that research and evidence do not exist in a vacuum but are powered by social relationships and interests [7]. This has implications for the role of researchers in the field. These issues are explored by Kapilashrami et al. who suggest that for researchers, engagement in social movements raises questions and challenges about remit, their own advocacy role and the potential for bias [3]. For researchers, engagement in studies of arts, health and well-being can spill over into advocacy-related work, risking perceptions of incorporation, with a loss of professional identity and status as well as de-legitimisation of research. Further difficulties can also arise when research findings appear to diverge with practitioner or community experiences. These concerns need to be balanced with a recognition that while robust methods are needed to provide transparency, the idea of research as independent, objective and neutral is something of a myth. Engaging in advocacy is increasingly recognised as part of the role of researchers. This is in part a consequence of recent trends towards demonstrating and valuing the impact beyond academia of publicly funded research. This encourages collaborative approaches that bring researchers, practitioners and stakeholders more closely together, creating genuine pathways through which research can have an impact on society. The arts, health and well-being field features many useful examples of this way of working, which accommodates close relationships with emergent practice while maintaining rigour and enabling critical perspectives to develop and be voiced.

To date, the bulk of research on arts, health and well-being has tended to examine the effects and impacts of arts in health and care, often seeking to identify health and well-being outcomes that resonate with national and local policy agendas, often in order to make the case for funding and support. In arts and health, questions about what works and what doesn't work, where outcomes are clearly identified, understood and agreed by stakeholders, are relatively easy to answer using established and improved methodologies. Broader questions raised by social movements, such as which concerns should be prioritised, how services should be funded, what determines the quality of arts and how do participants experience projects, are essentially political, moral, philosophical and aesthetic questions for which established scientific research methods cannot provide answers. This brief discussion of social movement theory supports the need for a broader arts, health and well-being research programme that draws on theories and methods from political and social sciences to address strategic questions that shape the development and impact of the field. It also serves as a reminder of the need for public participation in research and decision-making.

While there have been broad discussions about arts, health and well-being as a social movement, there have been few attempts to map or document the effects of sustained interactions between stakeholders within the field. This is a challenging topic as arts, health and well-being is made up of heterogeneous groupings with wide-ranging goals, and it may be difficult to establish causal links between stakeholder activity and observed changes in society. Nevertheless, given recent policy shifts towards recognising health as a social movement, understanding arts, health and well-being movement development, impacts and outcomes is a fruitful area for further research.

Conclusions

The diverse field of arts, health and well-being draws its energy from the work of a wide range of stakeholders including individual artists, project participants and researchers as well as small and large arts and cultural organisations. There is no single agenda driving arts, health and well-being as a social movement, but there has been a sustained practice of bringing together stakeholders in coordinating groups and networks in order to advocate for the field and influence power holders. This process has combined potentially disparate agendas into a broader programme that is sensitive to political opportunities and resources. Hence, alliances have been forged with leaders in the culture and health fields, and connections have been made with policy areas such as arts and culture, public health, management of long-term health conditions and new delivery models such as social prescribing. The field of arts, health and well-being bears some of the characteristics of a social movement, and it has followed trajectories documented in social movements, such as propagation of ideas and actions in what is an increasingly international field.

Social movements have historically made an important contribution to improvements in health and well-being, and there is still a strong need for them in order to address current health challenges and reduce inequalities. The notion of arts and health as a social movement is clearly aligned with current thinking that seeks to solve problems by harnessing grass-roots energies and developing new forms of leadership based on power sharing. Social movements vary in their sense of radicalism and grievance, with recent contributors advocating an energy-based perspective rather than one based on contentious politics. This emphasises the role that social movements play in healthy societies to foster collaboration in response to collective problems. However, social movements cannot be led from above, and there is a danger that they may exploit and sap the energy of the most vulnerable in society. Some would call for more radical agenda in arts, health and well-being that moves beyond convincing power holders of the role and value of arts and creativity. A more radical, bottom-up agenda, with an emphasis on capacity building at the grass-roots level, may be needed in order to challenge difficult political and economic issues.

Whether or not the diverse field of arts, health and well-being can be considered a social movement, social movement theory provides some useful insights that might help to guide further research and development. Research is needed to understand how to respond to organisational challenges such as propagation and scale and address pitfalls such as internal divisions and factionalism. Insights from social movement theory may also help to understand the paradoxes surrounding research and evidence in arts, health and well-being. Further work is needed to understand the way in which projects and programmes manage the trade-offs that arise from the need to balance the potentially conflicting goals of challenging dominant epistemologies and harnessing scientific evidence. Social movement theory challenges the notion of research as independent, objective and neutral. This highlights the need for public participation in research and decision-making and suggests that the social relationships and interests that drive research and evidence need to be made explicit.

Thinking about arts, health and well-being as a social movement provides a counterbalance to current research agendas dominated by quantitative methodologies and healthcare evaluation frameworks. It broadens the parameters of research, identifying critical questions about movement aims, vision, stakeholder interests, strategies and impacts. It allows exploration of the processes that shape outcomes, including processes of knowledge production and the power relationships that shape these. It could potentially enhance strategic awareness about the role of the arts in health and care, enabling stakeholders within both the arts/culture and the health/care fields to generate new knowledge about how to address challenges, including utilising evidence, working with scientific communities, shaping research agendas and influencing health and social care policy and practice.

References

1. Parkinson, C., *Devolution: The arts & health a social movement*. 2015, Manchester Metropolitan University. https://mcrmetropolis.uk/blog/devolution-the-arts-health-a-social-movement/
2. Royal Society for Public Health Working Group on Arts, H.a.W., *Arts, health and wellbeing beyond the millennium. How far have we come and where do we want to go?* 2013, London: RSPH. https://www.rsph.org.uk/resourceLibrary/arts-health-and-wellbeing-beyond-the-millennium-how-far-have-we-come-and-where-do-we-want-to-go-.html
3. Kapilashrami, A., Smith, K. E., Fustukian, S., Eltanani M. K., Laughlin, S., Robertson, T., Muir, J., Gallova, E. & Scandrett, E., *Social movements and public health advocacy in action: The UK People's Health Movement*. Journal of Public Health, 2015. **38**(3): p. 413–416.
4. Alasuutari, P. & Qadir, A., 'Social movements'. Chapter 6 in *Epistemic governance: Social change in the modern world*. London: Palgrave Macmillan, 2019.
5. Tilly, C., From interactions to outcomes in social movements, in *How social movements matter*, D. M. M. Giugni & C. Tilly (eds). 1999, Minneapolis and London: University of Minnesota Press. p. 253–270.
6. Brown, T. & Fee, E., *Social movements in health*. Annual Review of Public Health, 2014. **35**: p. 385–398.

7. Brown, P., Zavestoski, S., McCormick, S., Mayer, B., Morello-Frosch, R. & Gasior Altman, R., *Embodied health movements: Uncharted territory in social movement research.* Sociology of Health and Illness, 2004. **26**(1): p. 50–80.

8. Brown, P. & Zavestoski, S., *Social movements in health: An introduction.* Sociology of Health and Illness, 2004. **26**(6): p. 679–694.

9. McKeown, T., *The role of medicine: Dream, mirage or nemesis?* 1976, Princeton, NJ: Princeton University Press.

10. McGovern, L, Miller, G. & Hughes-Cromwick, P., *Health policy brief: The relative contribution of multiple determinants to health outcomes.* Health Affairs, August 21, 2014. doi:10.1377/hpb20140821.404487

11. Epstein, S., *The construction of lay expertise: AIDS activism and the forging of credibility in the reform of clinical trials.* Science, Technology and Human Values, 1995. **20**(4): p. 408–437.

12. Burbidge, I., *Releasing energy for change in our communities. Social movements in health.* 2017, London: Royal Society of Arts, Action and Research Centre.

13. del Castillo, J., Khan, H., Nicholas, L. & Finnis, A., *Health as a social movement. The power of people in movements.* 2016, London. www.nesta.org.uk

14. Arnold, S., Coote, A., Harrison, T., Scurrah, E. & Stephens, L., *Health as a social movement: Theory into practice, programme report.* 2018, London: Royal Society of Arts.

15. NHS England, *Five year forward view.* London. https://www.england.nhs.uk/publication/nhs-five-year-forward-view/

16. Guigni, M., How social movements matter: Past research, present problems, future developments, in *How social movements matter*, D. M. M. Giugni & C. Tilly (eds). 1999, Minneapolis and London University of Minnesota Press. p. xiii–xxxiii.

17. Christiansen, J., *Four stages of social movements.* EBSCO Research Starters, 2009.

18. Philipp, R., *Arts, health, and well-being: From the windsor conference to a Nuffield forum for the medical humanities.* 2002, The Nuffield: London.

19. Arts and Health South West, *Conference report, culture, health and wellbeing, Bristol 2013.* www.ahsw.org.uk/www.culturehealthwellbeing.org.uk

20. All Party Parliamentary Group on Arts, Health and Wellbeing, *Creative health: The arts for health and wellbeing.* 2017, London: APPG. www.artshealthandwellbeing.org.uk/appg/inquiry

21. Daykin, N. & Jos, T., *Arts for health and wellbeing: An evaluation framework.* PHE publications gateway number 2015595, London: Public Health England. https://www.gov.uk/government/publications/arts-for-health-and-wellbeing-an-evaluation-framework

22. Daykin, N., Willis, J., McCree, M. & Gray, K., *Creative and credible evaluation for arts, health and wellbeing: Opportunities and challenges of coproduction.* Arts and Health: An International Journal of Research, Policy and Practice, 2016. **9**(2): p. 123–138.

23. White, M., *A social tonic: The development of arts in community health.* 2009, Oxford: Radcliffe.
24. Parkinson, C., *Manifesto for arts and health*, Manchester: Manchester Metropolitan University. http://www.artsforhealth.org/manifesto/
25. de la Porta, D. & Diani, M., *Social movements: An introduction.* 2nd ed. 2006, Malden, MA: Blackwell Publishing.
26. Miller, F. D., The end of SDS and the emergence of weatherman: Demise through success, in *Waves of protest: Social movements since the sixties*, V. J. J. Freeman (ed). 1999, Lanham, MD: Rowman & Littlefield. p. 303–324.
27. Daykin, N., Mansfield, L., Payne, A., Kay, T., Meads, C., D'Innocenzo, G., Burnett, A., Dolan, P., Julier, G., Longworth, L. & Tomlinson, A., *What works for wellbeing in culture and sport? Report of a DELPHI process to support coproduction and establish principles and parameters of an evidence review.* Perspect Public Health, 2017. **137**(5): p. 281–288.
28. Feinstein, A. R., *An additional basic science for clinical medicine: 1. The limitations of randomised trials.* Annals of Internal Medicine, 1983. **99**: p. 544–550.
29. Levine, R. J., *Ethics and regulation of clinical research.* 1986, Baltimore, MD: Urban & Shchwarzenberg.
30. Fancourt, D. & Joss, T., *Aesop: A framework for developing and researching arts in health programmes.* Arts Health, 2015. **7**(1): p. 1–13.
31. Crossick, G. & Kaszynska, P., *Understanding the value of arts & culture The AHRC Cultural Value Project.* 2016, Swindon: Arts and Humanities Research Council.

6 Boundary work and boundary objects in arts, health and well-being

Introduction

The previous chapter suggested that social movement theory offers a useful lens with which to study the field of arts, health and well-being. As well as highlighting research challenges and development processes, social movement theory examines boundary work as a way of reducing divisions between groups, empowering marginalised voices, transforming identities and generating new knowledge. The study of boundaries, which can be physical and symbolic, has developed in organisational and educational research and has been applied to healthcare research organisations. Boundaries serve to demarcate areas of knowledge, tasks and disciplines, and their enforcement can lead to problems such as silo working. Sometimes, boundary crossing is needed to highlight shared concerns, encourage collaboration and help to bring about change and innovation in policy and practice. The study of boundary work is highly relevant to arts, health and well-being and could help to understand how the various groupings involved can work effectively together.

Boundary crossing in arts, health and well-being

Boundaries have been studied from the perspective of several academic disciplines including sociology, psychology and philosophy. Within the sociology of health and illness, boundaries have been viewed negatively in the context of competition for resources and professional protectionism. However, researchers have also examined the ways in which boundaries can be crossed in order to allow stakeholders with different expertise, interests and viewpoints to cooperate and work effectively together [1]. As increasing specialisation in healthcare has led to growing complexity and divisions, overcoming boundaries is recognised as a prerequisite of patient-centred care. The notion of boundary crossing captures the relationality of interdisciplinary work [2], which is central to arts, health and well-being.

Social movement theorists have identified boundary work as a key strategy that members of social movements use to engage with influential groups in society. While boundaries can be reinforced to limit the development and effectiveness of social movements, successful boundary crossing can reduce divisions such as those between specialisms, between expert and lay knowledge and between grass-roots and professional perspectives. Boundary work can create space between cultural practices for negotiation and empowerment of marginalised voices [3–8].

As boundary crossing is increasingly viewed as an effective response to current health and care challenges, interest has also focused on the role of people at the boundary. Boundary workers include care coordinators and link workers in social prescribing schemes who seek to build bridges between domains to support the delivery of integrated and person-centred care. Artists in healthcare settings also often act as boundary spanners, working across different domains and specialisms. Many arts projects in health and social care involve tactical boundary crossing, using artworks and processes to disrupt the symbolic boundaries that people create to demarcate people, objects and practices in order to make sense of the world [5]. Boundary crossing can take expressive forms, utilising artworks and performances in order to represent and pursue shared goals, creating affinities and building common identity across different groups. A boundary is usually distinguished from the territorial notion of a border, although the two terms are often used interchangeably [9]. Matarasso suggests that crossing borders or boundaries is a defining feature of interdisciplinary work in arts, health and well-being, which draws together diverse groups while highlighting the limitations of existing forms of organisation [10]. As boundary workers, whether the setting is a hospital, a community health setting, a mental health environment, a prison or a military setting, artists must build bridges, forge relationships of trust and navigate power relationships with a complex web of stakeholders. Yet artists are not necessarily prepared for this: they may be unfamiliar with the healthcare system, being drawn from the creative and cultural sector, itself demarcated by several fields such as visual arts, music and performing arts, each with its own history and professional identity issues.

Successful boundary crossing serves as a force for change, not just at the individual level and at the wider level of social practices. Few studies have examined the work of artists as boundary spanners in health and care contexts. However, researchers in organisational studies in health and education have explored experiences of boundary crossing or boundary spanning more generally, showing it to be a difficult and slow process that requires perseverance and time [2,3,8,11]. These authors emphasise boundary crossing as a two-way process, not a simple transfer of knowledge and information from one domain to another. Those who are successful in forging connections and facilitating communication across the various domains need to demonstrate leadership qualities of resilience, flexibility, strength of character. As well being able to understand the discourses and practices within the different domains, they need to be viewed as legitimate in the different worlds they seek to bridge. Observers of boundary spanning also emphasise barriers to successful outcomes, including professional resistance to perceived challenges to identity and status, differences in culture, knowledge and roles between different organisations, siloed training of health and social care professionals and lack of training and resources for boundary spanning roles.

Artists as boundary workers can experience ambiguity in their roles, reinforced by divisions of status, class, ethnicity and gender, and they can easily be marginalised in hierarchical healthcare organisations. They may be at risk from overload and excessive demands, and the concept of emotional labour, derived from Hochschild's 1983 study of flight attendants [12], has been applied to boundary work [13]. Emotional labour is defined as the effort to suppress 'inappropriate' emotions and/or elicit 'appropriate' emotions within oneself and/or others as dictated by the demands of a particular job. Emotional labour becomes more complex when working across boundaries, as boundary actors must be highly alert to variations in the need for impression management and the strategies likely to gain trust across a wide set of contexts [14]. For artists working in health and care, these issues can be heightened by their financially insecure and organisationally marginal positions; they are often engaged as freelancers on short-term projects. Further research is needed to understand the experiences of artists as boundary actors in health and social care.

Boundary objects in arts, health and well-being

It is not just people but also objects that cross boundaries. Boundary objects are artefacts or symbols that have distinctive meanings and uses in different contexts, but they are also recognisable across different worlds [1]. Boundary objects play an essential role in boundary crossing since they fulfil a bridging function as they travel across domains, reducing divisions allowing different interests to communicate and work together [2]. In social movement theory, boundary objects are utilised to make links and reduce divisions, such as those between lay and expert identities, as well as to support claims for resources and to recruit new members [6,7,15]. There are many examples of boundary objects in healthcare organisations including patient records, pathways, protocols and even patients [2,16]. The notion of cultural well-being has itself recently been explored as a boundary object [17]. Boundary objects in arts, health and well-being can include artists and artworks, participatory arts processes and participants, and creative practices. While few studies have examined artistic boundary objects in health and well-being, there are many examples of the use of boundary objects in these contexts. These include visual representations of the body and of medical procedures, often used to educate, to translate knowledge, to develop shared understanding between medical and lay perspectives, or to disrupt accepted conventions and identities, and to encourage new insights and reflections on the practice of medicine. Participatory arts activities also use boundary objects to reduce divisions between patient and professional identities, opening space for new representations of experiences of health and care.

Research on boundary objects in organisational contexts suggests that their success depends upon their ability to address specific needs and requirements of different users and their capacity to generate dialogue and new meaning. This interpretive flexibility is what allows boundary objects to successfully move back and forth between different sites, fostering collaboration [10]. However, not all boundary work is successful. Boundary objects can restrict as well as enable communication, and they can be dismissed as irrelevant if they fail to meet the needs and requirements of key stakeholders [18].

Mechanisms of boundary work in arts, health and well-being

Underlying mechanisms that shape the success or failure of boundary work have been identified including identification, coordination, reflection and transformation [11]. All of these operate in arts, health and well-being contexts, and awareness of them may help to interpret complex interactions between artists, clinicians, managers, patients, community participants and public citizens. The following sections include some suggestions for further research on the mechanisms, impacts and success factors for boundary work in arts, health and well-being.

Identification

Regarding identification, research on the use of artworks and artistic practices in boundary work could help to understand the ways in which these successfully highlight, delineate and challenge established identities and practices. For example, the role of artworks in illuminating lay and medical knowledge, highlighting divisions and affirming or challenging identities could be explored in ethnographic research. This could also identify instances where arts reinforce existing divisions, such as when artistic objects are used to communicate medical ideas to a presumedly uneducated lay public. While education is needed, this one-way process privileges scientific discourse over lay experience and may fail to connect with its target audience. Research could also explore processes of resistance to boundary work, such as when a proposed arts activity is rejected on the grounds that it might disrupt the workflow within a clinical setting.

Coordination

The impact of artistic objects and processes on communication and coordination could also be examined, for example, in research on the workings of multidisciplinary steering groups assembled to transform patient environments using commissioned and participatory arts. Attention should be paid to the communication issues that can affect boundary work, such as differences in language and culture that can exclude artists and lay people from decision-making. In our Creative and Credible study of evaluation in arts, health and well-being, artists expressed frustration regarding the language used in discussions about healthcare funding and commissioning. They were sometimes confused by the fact that the same words were being used by different stakeholders to convey quite different meanings [19]. While these issues are sometimes touched on in process evaluation, most research publications focus on benefits of arts projects, not the underlying mechanisms and processes that shape outcomes and impacts. Boundary work offers a useful focal point in this area, where theoretical frameworks are generally underdeveloped.

Reflection

Research should explore the extent to which boundary work encourages reflection, engaging participants in a creative and enriching process of meaning making that enhances their personal and professional worlds. Research is needed to understand the roles and experiences of artists and other boundary actors and stakeholders in arts and health contexts. There is an increasing body of qualitative research that explores participants' experiences and perceptions of arts activities in health and well-being contexts. However, to date, the experiences of artists and professionals have received lesser attention, and the notion of boundary work has rarely been applied in studies. A key issue is that of emotional labour: research is needed to understand its implications in boundary work in arts, health and well-being, which can be highly rewarding but can also lead to stress and burnout.

Transformation

Finally, research is needed to understand the transformatory effects of boundary work on the development of new tools, concepts and practices in arts, health and well-being. Artworks can successfully enhance the aesthetic dimensions of healthcare environments and even increase their capital value, but they may be weak boundary objects if this is their only function. In cases such as these, they may add a superficial sense of diversity, enhancing the positions of high-status occupants without inviting reflexivity or transformation.

Of relevance here is the ambiguous position of boundary actors, whose influence and authority can be undermined if they are viewed as peripheral and not really belonging to a particular domain or practice, and whose creativity, a necessary component of the role, may not easily mesh with the role requirements of traditional organisations [8].

As the above examples suggest, boundary objects are not always successful, and research is needed to understand the requirements for successful boundary work in arts, health and well-being. Examining the arts in health and well-being through the lens of boundary work and boundary crossing has the potential to enrich understanding of transformational change and its prerequisites in a wide variety of settings.

The Heart of the Matter

An example of a recent boundary spanning project in arts and health is The Heart of the Matter, created by artist Sofie Layton and bio-engineer Giovanni Biglino during Sofie's residency at Great Ormond Street Hospital (www.insidetheheart.org). The project drew together arts curators, producers and psychologists, with funding from UK charities and organisations. The project creates artworks based on the accounts of patients with heart conditions as well as scientists, artists, students and nurses, in order to reflect on the nature of the human heart. Inspired by stories and conversations, the work transforms medical images and uses patterns and rhythms produced by technologies such as magnetic resonance imaging (MRI) and computed tomography (CT) scans as the basis for the creation of artefacts using techniques such as 2D and 3D printing, digital animation, sound installations and sculpture.

The Heart of the Matter offers an example of boundary crossing that aims to support learning and transformation of health and arts domains. The project does not simply seek to educate the lay public about the complexities of medical care, as is the case in some traditional science education projects. Neither does it simply enhance the aesthetic environment. Rather, it seeks to challenge medical reductionism, resisting attempts to view patients primarily in terms of their clinical conditions. Hence, participants and observers are invited to consider the heart as an emotional and metaphorical object, to reflect on broader themes such as the preciousness of life, and to acknowledge the sacred dimensions of relationships and spaces where treatment and care take place.

The initial medical images that provide the basis of the creative work of The Heart the Matter are symbolic boundary objects that are clearly understood from different standpoints. Within the medical domain, they fulfil an information function, and within lay discourse, they are recognisable because of frequent representations of medical technology in popular media. From these objects, new artefacts are produced, a process in which meanings from art, medicine, technology and narrative are interwoven. Hence, the new artefacts don't 'belong' to a single domain: they possess interpretive flexibility that can both reinforce the world views of different users while also being capable of generating dialogue and new meaning across domains [1,11].

Case study: the role of boundary objects in music and dementia

The use of music, art, drama, dance and visits to museums and galleries with people with dementia has increased substantially in recent years. A growing evidence base suggests that participation in the arts can enhance health and well-being of people with dementia by stimulating creativity, promoting learning, aiding communication, triggering memories, increasing confidence, self-esteem and social participation, supporting and educating carers and challenging public perceptions of dementia [20–26]. There is considerable emphasis on music making for people with dementia, perhaps because of music's capacity to stimulate emotional and cognitive responses. A Finnish randomised trial reported that singing and music listening compared with usual care improved mood, orientation, attention, memory and quality of life in people with mild to moderate dementia in community settings [26].

Research on arts and dementia is characterised by several challenges. Arts projects in dementia care are often small and short term, limiting possibilities of evaluation. A key question is that of how to include the voices of people with dementia in research and programme development, since many studies rely on self-reporting and subjective indicators [25]. Research studies have tended to focus on people with mild to moderate dementia in community settings, hence understanding of the role of arts with people in the advanced stages of dementia or in hospital settings is less well developed. There are also practice challenges. Many projects emphasise the value of reminiscence for people with dementia, although this does not preclude the possibility of creativity and learning new skills through arts participation.

In an attempt to explore these issues, colleagues and I undertook a mixed methods evaluation of a weekly music activity for people with dementia in hospital [27]. Hospital environments can be stressful, frightening and confusing for people with dementia, compounding behavioural symptoms that are sometimes managed through overuse of antipsychotic drugs and contributing to poor clinical outcomes [28]. The music project sought to enhance the care environment, reducing stress, addressing agitation, contributing to clinical improvements and enhancing well-being for patients and staff. The activity was led by a professional musician who visited for a few hours each week, during which time he performed at patients' bedsides and, for those able to attend, facilitated a music making group in a side room close to the hospital wards. Participants were escorted to and from the session by staff, who helped with the session and served tea and biscuits. Participants joined in group activities which included singing familiar songs, using a conductor's baton to direct the musician as he played the viola, and improvising using hand percussion. The group also worked together under the guidance of the musician to compose new music and songs.

The research study compared ward environment data from the same two wards for two ten-week time periods, one when the music programme was being delivered and the equivalent period a year previously when there had been no music. One of the findings was a significant reduction in prescription of antipsychotic drugs during the music period, although several factors other than music could have contributed to this. Observations, interviews and focus groups with patients, visitors and staff involved in project delivery showed that participants and staff generally enjoyed the music making, which seemed to have a positive effect on the ward environment and on relationships.

The project revealed some of the complexities of delivering music activities for people with dementia in sensitive settings and high-lighted the role of the musician as a boundary spanner. Some challenges of the boundary crossing role in this context were apparent, for example, when a senior clinician interrupted a music participation session that was in full flow in order to carry out a routine clinical procedure on an individual who was taking part. Ultimately, some successful instances of boundary crossing and the use of boundary objects helped to enable successful outcomes for the project, over-coming divisions created by institutional hierarchies and from fac-tors that potentially constrained participants' engagement, including underlying health and mobility impairments as well as differences in musical backgrounds, experiences, preferences and beliefs. This was evident in the responses of front-line clinical and care staff, for whom the project created additional work, including recording consent, cap-turing clinical data, managing competing priorities such as protected mealtimes and the time-consuming task of escorting participants to and from the sessions. They generally showed great willingness to support patients and to protect the music time and space from incur-sions by more senior clinicians, although some expressed embarrass-ment when they thought they might be required to take part in music activities themselves.

The use of boundary objects such as musical instruments and a conductor's baton provided a strong focal point for discussions about patient care within the project, bringing professionals, researchers, carers and artists together to develop new insights. For example, as a boundary object, the conductor's baton carries powerful and distinc-tive meanings. In the world of music, the baton is a powerful symbol of authority and unity of the orchestra. When it was introduced into the healthcare environment and subjected to the regime of sterilisation, it quickly acquired a new meaning as a clinical object. Soon after, it was transformed to a symbol of empowerment, creativity and personhood as the patients were invited to take control of it, directing the musician to create sounds and textures that surprised and delighted all those tak-ing part, including patients, visitors, nurses, doctors and researchers.

In the focus group discussions that followed, professionals and carers expressed their surprise at the content of the project, particularly those elements involving composition, spontaneity and improvisation, as they had expected a greater emphasis on reminiscence. They were also surprised by the capacity of patients to engage in conducting and music making, and to engage, create and learn to a greater degree than they had initially assumed possible. Successful boundary work had helped them to gain knowledge and understanding of previously hidden patient stories, capabilities and needs as well as reflection on their own roles. These insights, together with the enjoyment of music, helped to nurture new perspectives about how to enhance patient care and improve the everyday working experiences of staff.

Conclusions

This chapter has explored the notion of boundary work in the context of arts, health and well-being, suggesting that processes connected with boundary crossing and boundary objects are highly relevant, although under researched, within the field. This focus on boundaries offers a useful theoretical framework for understanding the value and impact of a wide range of arts projects in health and well-being contexts.

Successful boundary work can reduce divisions based on identities, roles and organisational structures. As well as encouraging collaboration across disciplines, it can empower disadvantaged voices, creating new meanings and helping to bring about wider transformations in policy and practice. However, boundary crossing can fail, and unsuccessful boundary work can reinforce hierarchies, divisions and barriers to change. A clear focus on the mechanisms of boundary work, including identification, communication, reflection and transformation, could strengthen evaluation of arts for health and well-being, identifying prerequisites for success as well as risks and challenges for projects and collaborations.

Research is needed to understand the specific challenges faced by artists and other boundary actors in arts, health and well-being contexts, and the characteristics of boundary objects that can bridge domains and transform practice. Future research in this area could help to identify strategies and resources to support transformation, including systemic support, resources, management of professional identities and roles, training of artists as boundary spanners and support for the emotional labour of boundary work in arts, health and well-being.

References

1. Star, S. L. & Greisemer, J. R., *Institutional ecology, 'translations', and boundary objects: Amateurs and professionals in Berkeley's Museum of Vertebrate Zoology, 1907–1939.* Social Studies of Science, 1989. **19**: p. 387–420.
2. Cramer, H., Hughes, J., Johnson, R., Evans, M., Deaton, C., Timmis, A., Hemingway, H., Feder, G. & Featherstone, K., *'Who does this patient belong to?' Boundary work and the remaking of (NSTEMI) heart attack patients.* Sociology of Health and Illness, 2018. doi:10.1111/1467-9566.12778
3. Gilburt, H., *Supporting integration through new roles and working across boundaries.* 2016, London: King's Fund.
4. Gieryn, T., *Boundary-work and the demarcation of science from non-science.* American Sociological Review, 1983. **48**: p. 781–795.
5. Wang, D., Piazza, A. & Soule, S. A., *Boundary-spanning in social movements: Antecedents and outcomes.* Annual Review of Sociology, 2018. **44**: p. 167–187.
6. Epstein, S., *The construction of lay expertise: AIDS activism and the forging of credibility in the reform of clinical trials.* Science, Technology and Human Values, 1995. **20**(4): p. 408–437.
7. Edwards, R. & Fowler, Z., *Unsettling boundaries in making a space for research.* British Educational Research Journal, 2007. **33**: p. 107–123.
8. Aungst, H., Ruhe, M., Stange, K. C., Allan, T. M., Borawski, E. A., Drummond, C.K., Fischer, R. L., Fry, R., Kahana, E., Lalumandier, J. A., Mehlman, M. & Moore, S. M., *Boundary spanning and health: Invitation to a learning community.* London Journal of Primary Care, 2012. **4**(2): p. 109–115.
9. Jones, R., *Categories, borders and boundaries.* Progress in Human Geography, 2009. **33**(2): p. 174–189.
10. Matarasso, F., *A restless art. How participation won, and why it matters.* 2019, Lisbon and London: Calouste Gulbenkian Foundation.
11. Akkerman, S. & Bakker, A., *Boundary crossing and boundary objects.* Review of Educational Research, 2011. **81**(2): p. 132–169.
12. Hochschild, A. R., *The managed heart: Commercialization of human feeling.* 1983, Berkeley: University of California Press.
13. Needham, C., Mastracci, S. & Mangan, C., *The emotional labour of boundary spanning.* Journal of Integrated Care, 2017. **25**(4): p. 288–300.
14. Caldwell, D. & O'Reilly, C., *Boundary spanning and individual performance: The impact of self-monitoring.* Journal of Applied Psychology, 1982. **67**(1): p. 124–127.
15. Brown, P. & Zavestoski, S., *Social movements in health: An introduction.* Sociology of Health and Illness, 2004. **26**(6): p. 679–694.
16. Allen, D. A., *From boundary concept to boundary object: The practice and politics of care pathway development.* Social Science & Medicine, 2009. **69**(3): p. 354–361.

17. Daykin, N., Fast, H., Jaakonaho, L., Laukkanen, A., Lehikoinen, K. & Koivisto, T., *Cultural wellbeing as a boundary object.* Panel discussion, Nordic Arts and Health Conference, 21st May 2019, Clinical Research Centre, Lund University, Malmö, Sweden.
18. Laine, T., Korhonen, T., Suomala, P. & Rantamaa, A., *Boundary subjects and boundary objects in accounting fact construction and communication.* Qualitative Research in Accounting and Management, 2016. **3**: p. 303–329.
19. Daykin, N., Willis, J., McCree, M. & Gray, K., *Creative and credible evaluation for arts, health and wellbeing: Opportunities and challenges of coproduction.* Arts and Health: An International Journal of Research, Policy and Practice, 2016. **9**(2): p. 123–138.
20. Beard, R., *Arts therapies in dementia care: A systematic review.* Dementia, 2012. **11**: p. 633–656.
21. Pavlicevic, M., Wood, S., Powell, H., Graham, J., Sanderson, R., Millman, R. & Gibson, J., *The 'ripple effect': Towards researching improvisational music therapy in dementia care homes.* Dementia, 2015. **14**(5): p. 659–679.
22. Victor, C., Daykin, N., Mansfield, L., Payne, A., Grigsby Duffy, L., Lane, J., Julier, G., Tomlinson, A., & Meads, C., *Music, singing and wellbeing for adults living with dementia.* 2016, What Works Centre for Wellbeing. https://whatworkswellbeing.files.wordpress.com/2016/11/3-systematic-review-dementia-music-singing-wellbeing.pdf
23. Skingley, A. & Vella-Burrows, T., *Therapeutic effects of music and singing for older people.* Nursing Standard, 2010. **24**(19): p. 35–41.
24. Camic, P. M., Zeilig, H. & Crutch, S. J., *The arts and dementia: Emerging directions for theory, research and practice.* Dementia, 2018. **17**(6): p. 641–644.
25. Zeilig, H., Killick, J. & Fox, C., *The participative arts for people living with a dementia: A critical review.* International Journal of Ageing and Later Life, 2014. **9**(1): p. 7–34.
26. Särkämö, T., Tervaniemi, M., Laitinen, S., Numminen, A., Kurki, M., Johnson, J. K., & Rantanen, P., *Cognitive, emotional, and social benefits of regular musical activities in early dementia: Randomized controlled study.,* The Gerontologist, 2013. **54**(4): p. 634–650.
27. Daykin, N., Parry, B., Ball, K., Walters, D., Henry, A., Platten, B. & Hayden, R., *The role of participatory music making in supporting people with dementia in hospital environments.* Dementia (London), 2018. **17**(6): p. 686–701.
28. Dewing, J. & Dijk, S., *What is the current state of care for older people with dementia in general hospitals? A literature review.* Dementia, 2016. **15**(1): p. 106–124.

7 Conclusions and implications for future research

This book has reviewed the development of arts, health and well-being as an international field of research, policy and practice, suggesting that arts-based approaches can contribute to the transformation of health and care that is needed to meet future challenges. It has also identified some of the challenges involved in bringing 'arts' and 'health' together, drawing on sociological perspectives to identify political, organisational and social processes that create barriers and opportunities for change.

Research has increasingly demonstrated the health and well-being benefits across the life course of a wide variety of art forms, including music, visual arts, dance, drama and creative writing. Participation in arts and culture has been linked with improvements in individual health and well-being in a wide range of settings as well as wider benefits, including enhanced community cohesion and reduced social exclusion. Sustained advocacy and the growth of specialist resources and networks have contributed to the increased visibility of the field, along with policy shifts towards asset-based approaches such as social prescribing in health and care.

Despite these advances, a number of challenges remain. The development of the field continues to be uneven, with a concentration of arts-based knowledge and practice in relatively affluent countries. There are ongoing challenges surrounding research and evaluation of complex interventions such as arts. Research has tended to focus on positive aspects and on individual outcomes from arts activities and programmes rather than addressing broader questions about social impact. As well as evidence of outcomes, this book has considered research findings that provide insights into the processes that shape participants' experiences of arts in health and care. These include negative as well as positive experiences, as a key argument of this book has been that the benefits of arts and creativity should not be taken as a given but need to be understood in specific contexts shaped by macro-, meso- and micro-level forces. Issues of funding and resources have meant that the field has developed in a piecemeal and fragmented way, with a preponderance of short-term projects that rely on the energies of small organisations and individuals. The arts have been disproportionately affected by economic crises and macro-level policies of austerity, reinforcing unequal power relationships that limit collaborative working within health and care contexts.

The success of arts projects and programmes is also shaped by meso-level organisational structures and practices and by micro-level interactions and relationships, both of which are shaped by wider social divisions, discourses and relationships. For example, music and arts can represent valuable community assets, and there may be sensitivities to the misappropriation of these to meet policy agendas. Research is needed to understand the factors that foster and limit creative arts engagement in the context of widening inequalities. Research is also needed to understand the qualities and skills needed by arts leaders in order to address these challenges in health and care. For the field of arts, health and well-being to flourish, efforts are needed to develop capacity at the grass-roots level, as it is from this level that the energy of the movement is derived.

While the evidence base is growing, and further improvements in this area are needed, the development of the field is shaped by underlying questions that cannot be resolved by improved methodologies alone. Like arts, evidence does not speak for itself; issues of power, status and control over resources often lie behind debates about the type, level and amount of evidence that is needed to justify support for arts. The need for more and better evidence is not in question, but rather than advancing the case for evidence-based medicine, this book has turned to theoretical frameworks developed in social sciences and organisational studies to understand the future development, scope and impact of the field. Social movement theory is of relevance to arts, health and well-being because it highlights the political and moral nature of scientific questions and emphasises the need for user voices to be included in policy decisions. The field has often been described as a social movement, although relatively little attention has been paid to the implications of this. Social movement theory may help to shed light on key challenges including the paradoxical relationship that many within arts, health and well-being voice in relation to research and evidence, the tensions between radical and reformist agendas and the limitations of top-down leadership. Social movement theory may also illuminate questions about movement development, including issues of propagation and scale in relation to arts, health and well-being.

A related area is that of boundary work in arts, health and well-being. Recent thinking in health and care suggests that boundary crossing is a resource for learning and transformation. Objects as well as people can cross boundaries, and the study of boundary objects is highly salient in arts, health and well-being. As well as reducing divisions, boundary crossing projects can fail, and further research is needed to understand the specific challenges faced by artists and other boundary actors in arts, health and well-being contexts. The aim of this book is to stimulate new thinking about arts, health and well-being and to offer a counterbalance to current research agendas dominated by evidence-based medicine. Focusing on arts and health in terms of social movement theory and boundary work doesn't answer every need, but it broadens the parameters of research to include questions about vision and strategy as well as stakeholder motivations, interests and experiences. It has the potential to contribute to a broad research agenda that can guide strategic development and help to understand the role, scope and impact of arts in health and care.

Index

Note: Page numbers followed by "n" denote endnotes.